Fly Cheap!

FLY

CHEAP!

by
Kelly Monaghan

Fly Cheap!
✈ ✈ ✈

Published by:
The Intrepid Traveler
Post Office Box 438
New York, NY 10034, USA
http://www.intrepidtraveler.com

Copyright © 1999, 2001 by Kelly Monaghan
Second Edition
Printed in Canada
Book Jacket: George Foster, Foster & Foster, Inc.

Library of Congress Control Number: 00-132469
ISBN: 1-887140-16-6

Alternative Cataloging-in-Publication Data. Prepared by Sanford Berman, former Head Cataloguer, Hennepin County Library, Minnetonka, MN.

Monaghan, Kelly.
    Fly cheap. 2nd ed. New York, NY: Intrepid Traveler, copyright 2001.

    First ed. published 1999.
    PARTIAL CONTENTS: Foreword, by Rudy Maxa. —Frequent flyer miles. —Low-fare airlines. — Air passes. —Consolidators. —Air couriers. —Using the Internet. —Becoming a travel agent. —Further reading.
    1. Air lines--Rates. 2. Low-cost travel. 3. Travel agents--Vocational guidance. 4. Air travel--Costs. 5. Air courier travel. 6. Air travel--Internet resources. 7. Frequent flyer programs. 8. Air passes. 9. Consolidator tickets (Air travel).
    I. Title. II. Title: Cheap flying. III. Maxa, Rudy. IV. Intrepid Traveler.

387.712 or 910.202

Please Note

Although the author and the publisher have made every effort to ensure the completeness and accuracy of this guide, we assume no responsibility for omissions, inaccuracies, errors, or inconsistencies that may appear. Any slights of people or organizations are unintentional.

It must be understood that the listings in this guide in no way constitute an endorsement or guarantee on the part of the author or publisher. All readers who deal with the airlines and other companies listed herein do so at their own risk.

This book is sold with the understanding that neither the author nor the publisher are engaged in rendering legal or other professional advice. If legal or other expert assistance is required, the reader should consult with a competent professional.

The author and The Intrepid Traveler shall have neither liability nor responsibility to any person or entity with respect to any loss or damage caused, or alleged to be caused, directly or indirectly, by the information contained herein.

Bl

Table of Contents

Also by Kelly Monaghan

Air Courier Bargains:
How To Travel World-Wide For
Next To Nothing

Air Travel's Bargain Basement

Universal Studios Escape:
The Ultimate Guide to the
Ultimate Theme Park Adventure

Orlando's OTHER Theme Parks:
What To Do When You've Done Disney

Home-Based Travel Agent:
How To Cash In On The Exciting
NEW World Of Travel Marketing

The Intrepid Traveler's Complete Desk Reference
(co-author)

A Shopper's Guide To Independent Agent Opportunities
(co-author)

About the Author

KELLY MONAGHAN is a New York-based business and travel writer who began sharing his cost-saving travel strategies with readers with the book *Air Courier Bargains*. He is the author of *Home-Based Travel Agent*, which won a Recognition and Achievement Award from the Outside Sales Support Network, a professional organization of independent travel agents. Among his other books are *Universal Studios Escape: The Ultimate Guide to the Ultimate Theme Park Adventure* and *Orlando's OTHER Theme Parks: What To Do When You've Done Disney*.

In addition to his book writing, Kelly writes travel articles for magazines and ezines, including "The Intrepid Traveler Travels" (http://www.intrepidtraveler.com/travels). He also pens a monthly email newsletter for home-based travel agents (http://www.hometravelagency.com). As a corporate screenwriter, he has won a Cine Golden Eagle, a Telly, and both Gold and Silver Screen awards from the International Film and Video Festival.

Foreword

by Rudy Maxa

Buying an airline ticket seems like a haphazard exercise. Fares change by the second. An available deal might disappear in the ten minutes it takes you to consider booking it. Prices between airlines flying the same routes at the same time can vary widely.

What's going on here?

Well, first of all, there's very little random about the pricing of airline tickets, even though it can look that way to a consumer. As airlines and their computers have become more sophisticated in measuring the supply and demand for airline seats, pricing policies have become more precise. That's why fares change so quickly. A Boy Scout troop in Omaha decides to visit Washington, DC, and books 15 seats on a flight, and — bingo! — the remaining seats on that flight may suddenly become more expensive. The troop cancels its plans and fares may instantly fall on that particular flight, the better to entice someone else to buy a ticket.

There are general truisms, some with exceptions. For example, it's generally cheaper to book a roundtrip ticket two or three weeks before a flight. That's because airlines reserve their high-priced tickets for the last-minute business traveler. (In fact, the secret of the airline business in the U.S. is that it's the small number of passengers who pay full fare who make it possible for

15

leisure travelers who buy restricted, advance-purchase tickets to get such bargains.) So, is it ALWAYS cheaper to buy way ahead of time?

Well, not necessarily. Many airlines offer special weekend deals a few days before the flights. Their computers tell them which flights have too many empty seats. The airline then discounts these "city pairs" and sells them at a low price to anyone who's willing to abide by the special purchase rules — generally a Friday or Saturday departure with a return by midnight of the following Tuesday.

Then there are consolidator tickets to overseas (and a few domestic) destinations. You can often buy them a day or so before you travel and pay about the same fare as you would have if you'd booked them three weeks earlier. Why? Because major airlines quietly unload unsold tickets that way.

Confused yet? You should be. Even surveys of professional travel agents turn up widely varying ticket price quotes for the same routings. In short, it's a crapshoot out there.

Which is why you need to read this book.

Most travelers have no idea why the guy in the seat next to them paid $80 more or less than they did for their ticket. Most passengers don't know the difference between a consolidator ticket and a ticket on a scheduled charter flight. They don't know which ticket offers the greater flexibility at the better price. Which is why flyers should give thanks to Kelly Monaghan. For years — since he researched his first book about flying cheaply as an air courier — Kelly has been consumed with flying on the cheap. He knows the ins and outs of airline pricing, and where to find deals. Now he's put that knowledge into print.

Guys like Kelly and me spend entirely too much of our lives reading the small print at the bottom of airline ads and web sites. We really are genuinely interested in the nuances of airline pricing; our hearts leap when we find a new, low-cost carrier in Europe that no one on this side of the Atlantic has heard of.

Take advantage of this obsession. Buy this book. You'll not only validate Kelly's wretched life, but you'll save a lot of money in the future when you have to buy an airline ticket.

Introduction

In 1998, according to the Air Transport Association, America's airlines posted record-shattering net profits of $5.57 billion. That's net, not gross. In 1999, they pulled in $4.5 billion in net profits.

How did they pull this off?

Well, they raised prices for one thing, up a few percentage points each year. Part of it is luck. Until quite recently, jet fuel prices were at historic lows adjusted for inflation. And a generally robust economy has kept people flying.

But the airlines have generated a big chunk of their profits by mugging your travel agent.

Give a travel agent a hug

This book is designed to provide you with the knowledge you need to succeed in the never-ending battle to keep as much of your money as possible in your own pocket. So you might look on it as a do-it-yourself book. It might seem strange then that I'm starting off by proposing three cheers for your local travel agent.

Travel agents are a noble bunch. They provide a valuable service, the good ones at least, and they provide it for free. Until recently, that is. The airlines have been steadily whittling away at travel agents' ability to make a living by slamming them with a series of "cuts" and "caps." The commission percentage was cut (from an average 10% to 8% and then 5%) and the maximum commission paid limited to sums that make it virtually impossible for travel agents to eke out a slim profit. In some cases, the airlines will pay an agent just $10 for a booking.

Of course, the airlines didn't collude in this (perish the thought). And they certainly didn't fix prices in any way. (How dare anyone suggest such a thing!) It was just that in the spirit of the free market, they all just happened to do exactly the same thing at about the same time.

One result is that more and more agents have been forced to impose service fees to cover their costs. Wiser observers than I have noted that this is, in effect, a fare hike imposed by the airlines. Nonetheless, a remarkable number of travel agents continue to book airline tickets without imposing fees. Some have even declared that they will *never* charge a fee. Of course, some cynics predict that the airlines will eventually cut commissions to nothing. I'm afraid they may not be too far off the mark. When that happens, no travel agent will be able to sell air tickets for free and an invaluable source of unbiased information will be lost to the traveling public.

So, if you have a good, knowledgeable travel agent, rejoice. If you don't, find one. In spite of all the clever tips, techniques, and secrets I reveal in this book, I encourage you to nurture a lasting relationship with a good agent.

For one thing, many of the techniques in this book require the kind of in-depth know-how and day-to-day experience only a battle-scarred travel agent possesses. Even with fees, a good travel agent can save you money, especially if you are a business traveler facing those enormous fares the airlines love to charge for short, midweek trips.

One way to locate a good travel agent is to study the techniques in this book and then find an agent who knows how to put them into practice. For example, study up on codesharing practices and then see which agents know to book the cheaper alternative.

Once you have found a good agent, clasp him or her to your bosom with bands of steel. Give that person not just your heart-breaking, low-margin air fare business but your high-margin leisure business as well. A good travel agent can find you a terrific cruise or tour or independent fly-drive vacation that will be kind to your pocketbook, give you a great time, and still earn the agent a decent commission.

Remember that your time has a certain value and a travel agent, with his or her superior knowledge of the field, can save you tons of it.

Still, there are those of us who enjoy the thrill of the chase when the quarry is yet another super travel bargain to add to our trophy case. I suspect you are one of those people, because you are reading this book. Then, too, the airlines sometimes seem intent on wiping travel agents from the face of the earth. Given their superior firepower, they just might succeed. When that happens, we'll all be forced to live by our wits.

So, let's proceed.

Ready for takeoff

Snap quiz: Where do you live?

Okay, you did pretty well on that. But let's see how smart you *really* are? Which airlines fly from your local airport (or airports, for those of you in major markets)? Not so sure this time, were you?

The first step I am going to recommend is so simple that most people don't even think about it: Find out who flies from your local airport. If you are close to a number of airports, find out who flies from all of them.

If you are from a relatively small city, you may think you already know this information, but you may be surprised. Next time you travel, or when you drive Aunt Mary to the airport, take a few minutes to stroll the length of the terminal ticket counters and survey the airlines. Be on the lookout for the logos of minor airlines (maybe ones you've never heard of) lurking on the walls behind the ticket counters of bigger airlines. Many smaller airlines rent counter space from the big guys.

Next, find out where all these airlines fly to. An easy way to do that is to stop by the ticket counters and ask for a current schedule, or any other information they might have. Sometimes, you'll see flight schedules and brochures about frequent flyer programs and the like prominently displayed. Other times you'll have to ask. Surprisingly, to me at least, many airline ticket counters don't have any material at all.

Another way to get the information you're after is to ask for a copy of the latest issue of the airline's in-flight magazine. In it you are most likely to find its route map, an extremely valuable piece of information.

Take your booty home and file it away somewhere handy for future reference. Route maps make it especially easy to see where you can get to from where you are.

Another source of route maps is the Internet. Simply log onto an airline's web site and find its route map. Not all of them will have a route map posted, but if they do, you can simply print out that page. Unfortunately, this does not always produce the most readable image. Try setting your printer's controls to "grayscale" and see if that makes a difference in the quality of what prints out.

Another, better way is to copy the image of the route map. Not the whole page, just the graphic image that contains the route map. Then you can paste it into a page layout program, or even some newer word processing programs, enlarge it if necessary, and print it out.

If you live in a larger market, with several alternate airports within driving distance, collecting this information can be a bit tedious. Make it a game and do it a little at a time. If you are an inveterate traveler, you will find the file you compile will not only be useful but a lot of fun as well.

And now for the post-graduate test: Do you live in a low-fare or high-fare market?

Hands up everyone who said they live in a high-fare market. Good guess, but it's not quite that simple. While some markets have *generally* higher fares, the really important information is who has the best fares to where you want to fly. Fortunately, there's some pretty good information available on this topic and it's free from the government, another example of your tax dollars at work.

The Department of Transportation (DOT) publishes a quarterly *Domestic Airline Fares Consumer Report*. It takes them about three quarters to massage the data and publish each report so, given the rapidly changing air fare landscape, the report is never truly current. Still, it's a good start and, like I said, it's free. With this report in hand, you can locate, with a little difficulty, the city-pairs in which you are interested. A city pair is simply an air route between two cities. For each city pair, the DOT tells you the average fare, the airline with the biggest share of the market and its average fare, and the airline with the lowest average fare. Sometimes, the big guy in the market also has the best average fare, but often it's the airline with just a 10% market share that's offering the best deal. This kind of information is invaluable in telling you the best place to look for the best deal.

Just for the record, the latest report available as I am writing this showed that the highest-cost airports in the nation were Richmond, VA; Charleston, SC; Greensboro, NC; Charlotte, NC; and Rochester, NY. Travelers from Richmond paid a whopping 40 cents per mile, on average, to get where they had to go. The best places to live (as far as air fare goes, at least) were Providence, RI; Manchester, NH; Islip, NY; Las Vegas, NV; and Baltimore, MD. The good people of Providence paid just 11.6 cents per mile, on average, for their trips.

The easiest way to get hold of the latest report is to point your web browser to http://ostpxweb.dot.gov/aviation. You can also download the report's various tables in comma-delimited format; that, in turn, lets you sort the information any way you want, making it easier to find the city pairs that interest you the most. Also, each report has a "Special Feature" at the end, which varies from quarter to quarter, so you might want to download several reports. The Special Feature often focuses on low-fare airlines, a topic of special interest to readers of this book.

If you don't have access to the Internet (or the web site listed isn't working), you can request the report by calling (202) 366-1032.

Some notes on this book

The world of air fares is a complex one. In trying to sort through all the various permutations and combinations and present them in a logical fashion, I have made a primary distinction between the "major airlines" — America West, American, Continental, Delta, Northwest, TWA, United, US Airways — and everything else. My assumption is that, most of the time, when you fly you will either be flying on one of these airlines or between cities where one or more of the major airlines is an important factor. The first three chapters of the book then — *Ticketing Ploys, More Saving Ways,* and *Frequent Flyer Miles* — apply *primarily* to travel on the major airlines. From there, I lead you through the various alternatives to dealing directly with the major airlines: low-fare carriers, consolidators, air courier companies, and so forth. I wrap up things with a discussion of the Internet as a resource and research tool and the relatively arcane subject of serving as your own travel agent for fun and savings.

Ferinstances

Throughout this book I give examples to illustrate various points under discussion. Sometimes, the examples are clearly made up and so identified. Many times I use actual examples of real fares offered by real airlines. While these examples were true at the point in time they were gathered, they may not be true when you read this book. In fact, given the rapid-fire pace at which airlines change their fares and routes, it is highly unlikely that any example will be completely accurate in a few months time. The point is, I use the examples to illustrate *principles*. While the facts of the example might change, the principle should still hold true. So just because I illustrate Strategy A by telling how I found a $100 fare to City B on Airline C at some point in the past, doesn't mean you'll be able to get the same fare today. However, by using the same Strategy A, you should be able to get a very good fare to City D on Airline E. Or even to City B on Airline C.

Tickets vs. coupons

It will be helpful to understand the difference between a "ticket" and a "coupon," as the terms are used by the airlines. A ticket is a document, consisting of one or more coupons, issued to one person at one time. A coupon entitles the ticket bearer to a single plane ride, boarding at one point and deplaning at another. In other words, if you go to your local travel agent and buy a one-way trip from New York to Denver but the plane stops in Chicago en route, you have one ticket with one coupon. If, however, you go to the same travel agent and book a trip from New York to Denver with an overnight stay or a change of planes in Chicago, you have one ticket with two coupons. If you buy a roundtrip ticket from New York to Miami, you have one ticket with two coupons. On the other hand, if you fly one way from New York to Miami and then later purchase a one way ticket to return to New York, you will have purchased two tickets, each with one coupon. Got it? When taking advantage of many of the ploys discussed in this book, this is an important distinction.

The Internet

Later I debunk the myth that the best way — maybe the only way — to always get the lowest possible fare is to book it on the Internet. Nonetheless, the Internet is an amazing repository of information and, used knowledgeably, it can be a valuable resource for the budget traveler. Throughout this book I have listed appropriate web sites to assist you in your low fare quest. If you are not "on the 'Net," as the current saying has it, you might want to think about plugging in. In a few short years, a home computer with Internet access will seem as necessary as the telephone does today.

For your convenience, I have placed all of the links in this book on my own web site. Simply go there and you will have them all in one convenient jumping off place. The address is:

http://www.intrepidtraveler.com/flycheaplinks.html

Chapter One

Ticketing Ploys

Let's start with the basics. Some of this will seem screamingly obvious, but bear with me.

Premise Number One: An airline seat is a uniquely perishable product. Yesterday's bananas can be used for banana bread. Yesterday's airline seat is gone forever.

Premise Number Two: A full plane is more profitable than a half empty plane.

These two immutable truths have led the airlines over the years to devise any number of ingenious stratagems to sell the maximum number of seats possible on every flight before the witching hour — the moment the flight attendant slams the door — when, *poof!*, all their excess inventory disappears into thin air.

A corollary of this calculation is that margins in the airline business are on the low side (about six percent), so the more money you can get for each seat, the better off you're going to be. The goal then is to sell the maximum number of seats at the highest price possible. The result is the arcane science of "yield management," which I don't pretend to understand and won't even attempt to explain. Suffice it to say that the airlines have batteries of sophisticated computers, nurtured by (presumably) well-paid nerds who regularly feed them algorithmic goodies. These computers continually mull over the current state of the airlines' unsold inventory of seats and figure out how best to parcel out the remaining unsold seats at which prices to reach the desired goal of the fullest possible planes at the highest possible average price per seat. The result is not a single "best" fare but a bewildering variety of different fares, each one carefully hemmed in with restrictions and qualifiers and designed to capture a different segment of the flying public. Creating these many fares is possible because (in addition to having the computing power) the airlines have a great deal of information about our traveling and buying patterns.

Some of the calculations involved in yield management are fairly simple. For example, the airlines figure that if they give people a financial incentive to book early, they'll get a fair number of takers. This is the origin of those "supersaver" fares requiring 21, 14, or 7 days advance purchase. Not only does the airline have the use of your money for a period of time before having to actually deliver the goods (and since we're talking millions and millions of dollars here, a few days can make a difference), but there are also fewer seats to worry about selling.

Some of the calculations are devilishly clever. The airlines have taken note of the business traveler's penchant for dashing off on short notice to some distant city only to dash back as soon as whatever momentous task impelled the journey has been completed. According to one school of thought, the airlines took advantage of this peculiarity in the behavior of *homo commercialis* to charge outrageously high fares. The airlines, not surprisingly, see it differently. They point out that their frequent flights to popular destinations are designed to serve the business community (as opposed to the more flexible leisure traveler) and that, therefore, the business traveler should foot a higher portion of the bill for maintaining this infrastructure. If it weren't for the insatiable demands of the business community for next-second departures, the airlines would say, they could fill fewer flights to the hilt and charge lower prices. Well, maybe. There are certain undeniable financial incentives to make maximum use of the fleet; in other words, keep those planes in the air as much as possible, and that means more flights with more seats to fill.

The airlines have also noticed that business travelers like to get home by the weekend. In other words, their trips tend to begin on Monday or after and end on Friday or before. Leisure travelers, in contrast, tend to stay at least a week (the length of a fairly typical vacation). Even if their trips are shorter, the leisure traveler usually includes a weekend in his or her travel plans. Those two facts of business life — short notice travel and a desire to return home for the weekend — provide the airlines with the perfect recipe for nailing business travelers and making it virtually impossible for them to obtain a low fare. Even if John Q. Businessman buys his ticket weeks in advance, he is still required to stay over a Saturday night to qualify for the lowest fare. The lowest fares, called "excursion fares," are reserved for leisure travelers, defined as those who buy their tickets well in advance and stay over at least one Saturday night at their destination. And the fare difference isn't trivial either. The typical business fare (i.e. short notice and/or no Saturday stay) on many routes is *more than twice* the cost of the typical excursion fare for that very same route.

The airlines also realize that they are selling not just a seat on a plane, but a whole set of service intangibles attached to that seat. First class vs. coach is only the most obvious manifestation of this principle. In fact, the very same seat can have radically different intangibles attached to it. Some people (and again we're talking mainly about the business traveler) need a great deal of flexibility in their travel arrangements. If they are cutting deals left, right, and center in Denver, they might want to stay an extra day or at least take a later flight back. Or, if negotiations are at an impasse, they might want to make a dramatic exit and storm back to the airport. Consequently, they want tickets that can be easily changed, exchanged, or even refunded. The airlines take advantage of this fact by charging this traveler more for his ticket than they do the traveler who flies to Denver once a year to spend a week with Mom — even though on a given flight both travelers could be sitting next to one another. This, then, is the origin of "unrestricted" tickets, nonrefundable tickets, non-refundable-non-changeable tickets, and all the other variations on the theme.

Experience has also taught the airlines that people have favorite days to fly, with Monday, Friday, and the weekends being the most popular. As a result, flights that depart midweek tend to be cheaper. Again, there are two ways to look at this phenomenon: The airlines are soaking people who fly on high demand days, or they are subsidizing the less popular midweek schedules.

These factors and others get fed into the yield management hopper to be ground exceeding fine. The result is that on any given flight (ignoring for the moment the more obvious differences between first class and coach), the seats are sold at a variety of different fares, each carefully designed to get a slightly different segment of the traveling public on board and each subject to change on a daily basis as new information on how the flight is selling becomes available.

Things get more complicated when we factor in competition. Of course, the airlines are not supposed to collude or fix prices. That's against the law. Nonetheless they have managed to create something that looks, waddles, and quacks like a price-fixing duck without actually being one in the eyes of the law. What the airlines do is "chat" with each other via their computer reservations systems. One airline will, by posting a new fare on the system, say, in effect, "I'm thinking of raising the fare between X and Y to $500." If the other airlines think that's a good idea, they'll match the fare. If they don't match, the original airline will simply withdraw the fare. The same thing happens when lowering fares, so the occasional unmatched bargain can appear on the system for a brief time. Of course, the airlines aren't actually doing what I seem to be suggesting here. This is merely a hallucination on my part.

It might seem logical that the fare you pay would bear some direct relationship to the distance flown. Not so when competition is involved. A major airline might charge $80 to fly you 250 miles on a route on which it has a low-fare competitor, yet charge you $300 to fly you 225 miles on a route on which it has either no competition or which it shares with another major airline which "just happens" to charge the same $300.

In keeping with the free market and the spirit of competition, various airlines have moved to control certain markets by utilizing the "hub and spoke" concept. This means that an airline sets up shop in a conveniently located major city (the hub) and then runs most of its flights to other cities from there. The resulting route map shows lines radiating out from the hub to other cities like spokes on a bicycle wheel, hence the term. Such an arrangement offers undeniable economies and efficiencies for the airline as well as convenience for people who live near the hub. It also creates some bizarre fares.

For example, if you fly nonstop into Major Airline's hub city, you might pay a fare of $300 (to pick an arbitrary amount for the sake of discussion). But suppose you want to fly to City B on the other side of the hub city. Major Airline will fly you there with a stop, and maybe a change of plane, in its hub. You might think this second itinerary will cost more. After all, City B is farther away than the hub, the airplane therefore flies farther consuming more fuel, you get another bag of peanuts, another free Coke, and so on. Yet it is very likely that the fare to City B will be *less* than the fare to the hub, say $275. Why? Perhaps there is less traffic between the hub and City B and Major Airline wants to increase its load factor on that route. Or maybe one of Major Airline's competitors can fly you directly to City B and Major Airline can't. So Major Airline sets its fare to City B to match or beat its competitor's fare. The airlines know this sort of thing works because their computers tell them so.

You might be wondering exactly *how* the airlines figure all this out. Well, thanks to the popularity of frequent flyer programs it's no problem at all. Your frequent flyer number is a unique identifier. So the airlines have been tracking your travel patterns for years now, much as a scientist keeps track of hundreds of seemingly identical white mice by shaving a patch of their fur and tattooing a number on their skin. Think about it.

In summary, then, air fares are influenced by several main factors:

In general, fares are affected by the airline's need to make a profit. The only time an airline will price a route below break-even is when it is engaged in predatory pricing to drive a competitor out of business. Except, of course, airlines *never* do this.

On a given route, fares are shaped by market demand and competition. If there is little or no competition on a route, the airline will be torn between capitalizing on its monopoly and setting fares at a level that will fill the most seats. When there is competition, the airlines usually manage to keep their fares within a dollar or two of each other — low-fare airlines and fare wars being the wild cards in this particular game.

On a given flight, fares are determined by the public's travel patterns. As you probably know, there seem to be as many different fares in coach as there are seats. That's because the airlines' yield management computers and the wizards behind them have devised all of the devilish restrictions and stratagems mentioned above and many more to ensure that they squeeze the highest possible fare out of everyone on the plane, without driving you into the arms of competitors.

The challenge is to tiptoe through the yield management mine field to arrive safely at the lowest possible fare. Navigating successfully requires a fair bit of knowledge and the mastery of a grab bag of ticketing ploys. That's what this chapter is all about.

As you read on, bear in mind that these ticketing ploys apply (by and large) to the major airlines, which most of us use most of the time. Later chapters on frequent flyer miles, low-fare airlines, consolidators, and air couriers will enlighten you on other ways to fly cheap.

Ploy #1: Book early

Well, *duh!*

I almost didn't put this one in because it's so obvious and the booking strategy with which most people are familiar. Still, it's worth remembering that the so-called supersaver fares require advance booking. So if your schedule permits it, by all means buy your tickets early.

Remember, too, that there are several advance purchase deadlines. The most common ones are 30, 21, 14, 7, and 3 days. Most airlines will have more than one advance purchase fare for any given route; so as soon as you know you're going, it's wise to book. I've had too many friends call up to moan that they'd put off buying tickets only to discover that the deadline was yesterday and ask what to do now.

Advance purchase restrictions are most common (and most costly if missed) with the major airlines. However, they also apply to some low-fare airlines (see Chapter Four). Some other low-fare airlines have no specific advance purchase deadlines, but allot blocks of seats at different prices on a first-come, first-served basis. Either way, the earlier you book the better.

Jump on fare wars and sales

Booking early may not be as self-evident in the case of airline fare wars and limited-time-only sales. However, depending on the circumstances these events can offer opportunities for the farsighted budget traveler.

For example, suppose you fly to Kansas City every November for a cherished niece's birthday. You pick up the paper on a chilly January day and discover that the airline you usually fly has announced a sale. (The press does an excellent job of publicizing the airlines' sales and ignoring their price increases.) "Too bad," you think, "It only lasts a week." However, the terms of the sale may be that you must book and buy your ticket immediately, but the travel can take place much later. It's a golden opportunity to lock in a bargain fare for a trip you know you'll take. Depending on the rules attached to sale fares, this might also be a good time to buy in bulk (see Ploy #2). For more on tracking fare wars and sales, see Chapter Two.

Ploy #2: Buy in bulk

Selling (and buying) in bulk is a time-honored retail tradition. A dozen eggs costs less on a per-egg basis than three. The same can apply to airline tickets, and many airlines do offer bulk discounts from time to time, a book of ten coupons for the price of nine, for example. A consortium of 16 of the smaller European airlines with destinations in 26 countries offers an attractive Air Pass program that lets you fly individual segments for $99 per flight (see Chapter Five). Be alert to such special offers and take advantage of them.

A lesser known wrinkle in airline rules offers similar bulk buying possibilities. It requires knowing a great fare when you see one (your travel agent can help) and then jumping on it before the airline changes its mind. It also requires knowing the rules attached to a given fare.

Airlines often offer attractive fares, usually as weapons in a fare war. The idea is to grab a little market share (or perhaps drive a low-cost competitor out of business) and then jack the fare back up again. The fares offered during fare wars are time-limited; they are good for a month or so and then all bets are off.

But every now and then an airline will announce an "unrestricted" fare (i.e. no minimum stay requirement) with a great price and (here's the key) no expiration date. That enables you, the consumer, to lock in that great fare for as many trips as you'd like for a full year — even if you're not sure when you'll be flying. (Even though the fare has "no expiration date," airlines seldom like to book more than a year out.) Here's how it works:

Let's say Northwest announces a great fare of $119 from Kansas City to Detroit (as it did once). Let's say, also, that you live in KC but have family in Motown. You go there several times a year. Get your travel agent to book you *one ticket* with as many coupons as you'd like flights. The ticket will read KC-Detroit-KC-Detroit-KC-Detroit-KC and so forth for as many roundtrips as you'd like to take. The ticket will cost $119, times as many roundtrips as you want.

The best part is you don't have to lock yourself into specific dates. The only date that has to be on the ticket is on the first coupon. You have to take this flight. Of course, in practice you'd probably also know your return date on the first trip to Detroit. You can leave the dates "open" on the remaining coupons. When you decide when you want to fly, just call the airline and book the flight. No extra charge. You are protected from fare increases — even if the airline cancels the fare code under which you booked.

There are exceptions to the open segment rule. Sometimes fares with no expiration date will also prohibit open segments. Then, you'll have to book all segments for specific dates. Of course, you can use this ploy with fare war fares, too. You'll just have to complete all your trips within the time restrictions announced along with the fare war. Typically, in these cases, all travel must be completed within several months.

Note: This ploy works just as well for family travel as it does for business travel.

Ploy #3: Time your travel well

As every experienced traveler knows, when you travel can make a big difference in how much money you pay to get wherever it is you're going. If you can be flexible in your timing, you can often realize big savings.

Seasonal fares

Perhaps the most obvious example of this principle is the fluctuation in air fares with the seasons. Travel in the "high season" always costs more than travel in the "low season." There is a third category, called the "shoulder season," which is a fairly arbitrary period of time between high and low seasons during which fares descend or rise in stages.

Worth bearing in mind is that the "seasons" vary by destination. Summer is very definitely the high season in Europe, but it is the low season in the Caribbean. Leisure travelers who are able (or perhaps more to the point, willing) to take a contrarian position can realize substantial savings simply by touring at times when the tourist hordes thin out.

Holiday periods are high season everywhere and yet they offer some opportunities for the truly flexible flyer. Christmas day and Thanksgiving day are probably the slowest days of the year in the airline business, so if you are enough of a curmudgeon to turn your back on friends and family and fly on those days, you can snare some real bargains.

Midweek

Most travelers fly early in the week or at the weekend. Air fares reflect this pattern by offering incentives to fly in the middle of the week. In general, fares Tuesday through Thursday will be cheaper, with the cheapest likely to be for flights departing on Wednesday and Thursday.

Off hours

The same principle holds true for times of the day. After all, who wants to fly at the crack of dawn or late, late at night? But there are flights at those times and they are priced to reflect the low load factor. If you can rise before dawn, ask the airlines what they have available between 5:00 a.m. and 8:30 a.m. on the days you're traveling. If you can travel late at night, especially from West to East Coast, inquire about late night "red-eye" flights. Truly hardy souls can use the transcontinental red-eye not only to save on air fare but to save the cost of a night in a hotel as well.

Ploy #4: Purchase a package

If your trip plans include a rental car and a hotel stay, consider the savings potential of what the travel industry calls a "package." A package is simply two or more separate travel "products" (an airline ticket, a rental car, a hotel room) bundled together and sold at a single price. It's another way of buying in bulk and follows the time-honored retail tradition of rewarding those who buy several items with a discount.

Packages of this sort are put together by tour operators or "packagers" who negotiate with the various suppliers to purchase the individual package elements at wholesale prices, thus enabling them to offer the package at an attractive price. A package might include air fare and a rental car, air fare and a hotel, air fare and both a rental car and hotel, or all three plus a guided tour of the destination city. Packages can also include things such as admission to attractions and discount coupons to local restaurants.

Another thing that makes packages attractive to the budget traveler is that they are often free of the advance purchase requirements attached to airline tickets. In other words, the price of an airline ticket alone to, say, Nashville might be cheaper on the 15th day before flight time than on the 13th day, whereas a city package to Nashville might cost the same on both days. In fact, some of the tour operations of major U.S. airlines require advance purchases of just three or four days. Most packages will require a minimum stay of at least two nights, with three or four nights being more common.

City packages or fly/drives (as these products are sometimes called) are not available to every destination. Or at least they are not available *cheaply* to every destination. However, if your destination is a major city like New York, Chicago, or Los Angeles you should have no trouble locating an attractively priced package. The same holds true of smaller cities with a regular tourist trade (Orlando, Nashville, Branson, Missouri, and so forth) and major international destinations.

Here are a few additional things to bear in mind about city packages:

- City packages, like most tour products, are priced on a double occupancy basis. Some airlines require two people on every booking (at least to certain destinations). In other situations, solo travelers may have to pay a premium, but should still wind up saving money.
- A package from a major airline will not invariably be the cheapest alternative, especially if you are the kind of budget traveler who flies a low-fare airline and is willing to stay in the no-name, 40-year-old motel out of town or an inner-city youth hostel. Those who prefer "brand name" rental cars and hotels, however, should do quite well.
- Some packages may require a Saturday night stay. Those that don't will be especially attractive to business travelers.

Conveniently enough, most airlines have created their own in-house tour operations that may be able to offer you a package to your destination. However, most of these in-house packagers operate separately from the main reservations department and have their own toll-free numbers.

Air Canada Vacations (800) 774-8993
Alaska Airlines Vacations (800) 468-2248
America West Vacations (800) 356-6611
American Airlines Vacations (800) 321-2121
British Airways Holidays (800) 247-9297
Continental Airlines Vacations (800) 634-5555
Delta Vacations (800) 872-7786
Midway Vacations (800) 996-4392
Northwest World Vacations (800) 727-1111
Southwest Vacations (800) 423-5683
TWA Getaway Vacations (800) 438-2929
United Vacations (800) 328-6877

US Airways Vacations (800) 455-0123
Virgin Atlantic Vacations (888) 937-8474
In addition to the airlines, a great many independent tour operators offer city packages and fly/drives. Here are two of them.
Adventure Tours USA (800) 999-9046
City Escapes (800) 222-0022
Many tour operators will not deal directly with the general public, so you may have to go through a travel agent. A good travel agent will be helpful in locating the best packager for your target destination.

A final note

Those of you who function as your own travel agent (see Chapter Nine) will find packages especially attractive since they offer much more generous commissions than do airline tickets alone. Home-based travel agents should check with their host agency to see which preferred suppliers offer packages. If your host agency is getting a 15% commission and you are receiving 70% of the commission, that's like getting an additional 10.5% discount on the already low package price.

Ploy #5: Split tickets

Many times you will find that if you are willing to accept a trade-off on convenience, you can save some money by "splitting" your trip into two flights, changing planes at some intermediate point. Typically, this ploy will also involve using a low-cost carrier for one or both segments (see Chapter Four).

For example, a roundtrip from Kansas City to Albuquerque on a major airline will usually cost more than flying via Denver on Frontier.

Flying a major airline from just about anywhere east of the Rockies to Las Vegas and switching to Southwest or another carrier for the quick hop over to California will invariably be cheaper than a nonstop flight directly to your California destination. (It'll also give you a chance to lose your savings in the Vegas airport's slot machines!)

This ploy also works on the same airline for selected itineraries. For example, a major airline recently offered a $1,040 non-stop fare from Atlanta to Honolulu. But by making a connection in Los Angeles on the same airline, you could save $287. The same thing applied from Boston; in this case, the savings was $284.

Split the journey as well as the ticket

As long as you're going to be changing planes in Chicago (or Atlanta, or Dallas), why not stay awhile? Use the opportunity to visit friends or treat yourself to a mini-vacation on the way back from a business trip. Sometimes you don't even need to stay overnight. Businesspeople are not averse to "taking a meeting" at the airport if there is a valid reason to see you.

Harried businesspeople can also use the split ticket ploy to save some wear and tear on the system and perhaps some money as well. Let's say you have to fly to a distant city for a 10:30 a.m. meeting. Most people will plan to fly there the night before, after business hours, get to a hotel at some ungodly hour, take the meeting the next morning, and fly home in the afternoon. Instead, why not fly to some intermediate point, preferably a major hub, the night before, check into an airport hotel at a decent hour, and continue the journey the next morning in time to reach the meeting? Whether or not you'll save money depends on the circumstances, the routing, and the airlines involved, but run this idea past a crack travel agent next time you need to take a business trip and see what your options are.

Ploy #6: Find a fare, find a flight

First, some background: The airlines keep track of their kaleidoscope of fares by assigning each discreet fare a "fare code." KE21NR is an example of such a code. The fare code in turn is linked to lengthy "fare rules" that spell out in detail the restrictions and conditions that make this fare different from all other fares and enable the airline to answer the question, "Why did the guy sitting next to me pay $250 less for his ticket than I did?"

As the term suggests, a fare code is a cryptic way of summarizing the fare rules. The first letter in every fare code identifies the "class." The most obvious classes are first (F), business (C), and coach (Y). Actually, Y refers to so-called "full-fare coach," which is the most expensive, unrestricted coach fare. There are many other classes in coach, with B, H, K, L, M, Q, S, and V being the most common letters used. However, different airlines assign different class codes, so you may encounter others.

The large number of classes gives you some idea how thinly the fare pie is sliced by the boys in yield management. Of course, there will often be more than one fare in any given class as determined by the restrictions in the fare rules.

The letters and numbers that follow the class designator sketch out the major restrictions and conditions. For example, the fare code KE21NR tells those in the know that this fare is in K class, is an excursion fare (requiring a Saturday night stay), requires a 21-day advance purchase, and is nonrefundable. Nonrefundable can also be indicated by the letter N. So KE14N would mean a nonrefundable excursion fare requiring a 14-day advance purchase.

If you pay attention to fare codes, compare the codes to the rules, and ask questions of airline reservationists, you will gradually develop the skill of interpreting these codes. I provide some more examples below.

Using fare codes

Now that you know a bit about fare codes, what can you do with them? Well, the Internet makes it fairly easy to locate the lowest published fares between any two cities. You can then print out the detailed fare rules attached to this rock-bottom fare. This is valuable information for budget travelers, especially those who can be flexible. Allow me to illustrate.

Let's say I decide to fly from Phoenix to Cleveland on a Thursday three weeks from now and return the following Thursday. I call my travel agent, ask for the lowest fare, and am quoted $238 roundtrip. But if I turn to the Internet first, I will discover that the lowest published fare between Phoenix and Cleveland is just $198 and it's offered by six different airlines. (Isn't it an amazing coincidence that all six airlines just happen to offer precisely the same fare? And with almost precisely the same fare rules? Pure coincidence, of course.) So why didn't my trusty travel agent get me that fare?

The answer is simple: To get the lower fare I would have to fly, in both directions, on a Tuesday or Wednesday. The fare rules tell me this. Since I am a flexible traveler, I can easily arrange to fly out and back on Wednesday instead of Thursday and save $40. (The lesson to be learned here, by the way, is to alert your travel agent when you can be flexible on dates to save on the fare. This is also a good reason to find a regular travel agent who will become familiar with your travel patterns and your likes and dislikes.)

Sometimes it's not that simple. For example, I found a fare of $178 between New York and Albuquerque on America West, but when I tried to book flights on the Internet and, then, directly with the airline, the best I could get was a fare of $482 with a connection in Houston. However, because I was armed with the fare code and fare rules for the $178 fare (printed out from the Internet), I was able to work with the airline reservationist until she was able to figure out how to get me that fare. It turned out that to qualify for the fare I had to make a less convenient connection via Phoenix.

Sometimes, you will be disappointed. Fares expire. The seats allocated to a particular fare get sold out. Of course, in the Phoenix-Cleveland scenario sketched out above, if you couldn't get the fare on your first-choice airline, you'd have five others from which to choose. By the way, since this kind of fare code research shows you all the airlines serving the city pair in which you're interested, you can often decide which airline to use based on secondary considerations such as schedule or which will give you the most needed frequent flyer miles.

The point is that, when you have the fare, the fare code, and the fare rules in hand, you have some power. Not with the Internet booking engines (of which more later), because they are dumb machines, but with travel agents and airline reservationists. It can take an experienced travel agent to match a fare code to an itinerary, which makes situations like this a good way to "test" agents and help you identify the real pros. Airline reservationists will not always immediately recognize a fare as valid between two cities on given dates. My impression is that their computer systems default to the "simplest" way of getting you from Point A to Point B and not necessarily the cheapest way. But, since you can cite the fare code and quote from the rules, they will keep looking. Otherwise, they might simply insist they had already provided you with the lowest fare.

In Chapter Eight, I explain ways to use the Internet to do this type of lowest fare research, as well as debunk the myth that the Internet invariably finds you the lowest fare. For the moment, just take my word for it that this information is easy to come by. There is one important exception, however. If two cities are connected by a low-fare airline whose fares are not listed in the computerized reservations system used by your Internet source, it is possible that the low-fare carrier might have a fare even lower than the "lowest" fare you find on the Internet.

More on fare codes

Remember, fare codes only summarize the main restrictions associated with the fare. To get the full picture you will have to read the rules themselves which can be quite lengthy, not to mention hard to decipher. Another important point to bear in mind is that neither fare codes nor fare rules can tell you on precisely which flights a particular fare will work.

Here are some other common indicators that appear in fare codes *after* the first letter:

X = Usually appearing in the second position, indicates travel must occur Monday through Thursday, usually in both directions.

Y = When Y appears in the second position it usually indicates that travel must take place Friday through Sunday. Not to be confused with the full-fare coach class indicator.

N = When it appears in second position, usually indicates the fare is available only on a night flight. At the end of the code it tends to indicate a nonrefundable fare.

AS, CS, COM = Indicates a companion fare; typically one passenger flies "free," paying only taxes and Passenger Facility Charges (PFCs).

IP = Instant purchase. Another way of saying "nonrefundable."

25, 50, 75 = At the end of a fare code, these numbers indicate the percentage penalty you incur when you cancel. In other words, if the code is 25, you get back 75% of the fare if you cancel.

Ploy #7: Book international, fly domestic

The airlines' efforts to build market share sometimes result in fare structures that allow you to pay less for buying more. That may sound like a hidden city ploy (see Ploy #13), but the fares we're about to discuss do *not* involve hidden cities. Typically they use the airlines' so-called "circle fare" pricing or stopover rules to produce savings. If you really can't or don't want to take the extra trip, don't. Just enjoy the savings. They might not be as great as those realized with generally prohibited back-to-back ticketing (see Ploy #14), but you won't break any rules.

This ploy involves adding an international segment (or sometimes a trip to Hawaii) when you are purchasing a ticket for a short turnaround business trip. Because your business trip must be purchased at a sky-high price, you can take advantage of some of the sweeteners the airlines offer to those who are paying top dollar.

When you can use this ploy, which destinations you can use and how much you'll have to pay will depend on what the various airlines are offering at the time you travel. A knowledgeable travel agent will be extremely helpful in this regard.

A few actual examples will illustrate how this ploy works. Bear in mind that these ferinstances, culled from Terry Trippler's discontinued and much missed *Airfare Report*, were true at one point in time. It is unlikely that you will be able to find precisely the same deals today. Nonetheless, the principle remains the same and similar deals can be found, either by asking the right questions of the airlines or, again, by using a good travel agent.

A West Coast example

You have to fly from Los Angeles to Washington, DC, for a few days. Instead of booking a straight roundtrip ticket at $1,392, you have your travel agent get you one ticket with four coupons: LA-Washington-LA-Honolulu-Los Angeles. The fare? $907, a savings of $485. In this example, the Honolulu trip had to take place within 60 days of the return to Los Angeles. Not only does our business traveler save money, but the airline throws in a "free" trip to Hawaii. Even better, at the time this example was available, it was possible to take a companion to Hawaii for an additional $402 — still less money than the cost of a short roundtrip to DC by itself.

Some East Coast examples

A Philadelphia business traveler is going to Phoenix for a few days. The unrestricted coach fare is $1,325. Instead, the traveler gets a ticket adding Bermuda within 60 days of the return to Philly, saving herself about $18 — not a lot of money, granted, but she gets a free trip to Bermuda to boot.

Or consider the Boston businessperson flying to LA for a few days. That person could also get a Boston-Hawaii trip booked at the same time on the same ticket for $102 less than the cost of the LA trip alone.

A business traveler in Atlanta wasn't quite as fortunate. This person flew to California on business and booked a trip to Bermuda on the back end. The total fare was $14 more than the California trip alone, but when was the last time you got a roundtrip ticket to *anywhere* for $14?

Here's another Trippler technique, as reported in *Travel Weekly*. A businessman faces a whopping $1,665 fare to fly from Newark to Houston in coach in December. But he is also planning another short business trip, in business class, to Frankfurt in January, for the princely sum of $5,224. The total cost of both trips is $6,889. He decides to exploit the airline's rule allowing free stopovers on international business fare flights. He does this by buying a one way ticket to Houston ($834). He then has his travel agent write his business class trip to Frankfurt as follows:

Houston-Newark-Frankfurt-Newark ($5,424). He returns from the Houston trip, enjoys his "free" stopover, and then flies to Frankfurt a few weeks later. The net/net on this deal is that his total out-of-pocket is now $6,258, a savings of $631. Even better is that (again, thanks to the rules governing international business class fares) he gets to fly the Houston-Newark leg in first class.

A Midwest example

A Detroit business traveler is looking at a two-day trip to San Francisco. By booking an open ticket to Frankfurt at the same time, she pays $767 more. But she gets an unrestricted ticket (i.e. no minimum stay requirements) to Frankfurt for $568 less than it would otherwise have cost. And she doesn't have to lock herself into specific dates; she can use those open coupons any time within the year. Of course, if this traveler is interested in a *vacation* trip to Europe, she might be able to do better than $767 using a consolidator or a tour package.

Final thoughts

As you can see from the above examples, you won't always be able to save money using this ploy; you may actually pay a bit more. But in exchange you'll get an extra trip at a very low cost. Unfortunately, this ploy has limited application for the leisure or budget traveler. However, there comes a time when those of us who would never dream of flying coast to coast for just a few days will be forced to do so. When that happens to you remember this ploy. It could soften the financial blow.

Ploy #8: Pick the right airport

Because of competitive pressures, introductory fares on new routes, or the presence of a low-cost carrier in a particular market, air fares to and from cities that are quite close to one another can vary significantly. By carefully choosing your airport, it is possible to trade a small difference in miles for big savings.

For example, unrestricted fares (without a weekend stay) from the West Coast to Detroit once ranged from $1,278 to $1,342. But it was possible to fly to Toledo, Ohio, just 50 miles from Detroit, for as little as $334 to $344 with a 21-day advance purchase. Even at the 7-day advance purchase fare, the most expensive trip to Toledo was only $752. More recently, it was possible to fly at the last-minute to Detroit for just $802, but you could still reach Toledo for less — $630. So why not fly into Toledo and rent a car (which you'll probably need anyway) for that 50-mile jaunt into the Motor City?

Similar savings could be realized when choosing Birmingham, AL, over Montgomery (less than 100 miles away). From Denver, the difference was $606, from Dallas, $478.

On the East Coast, a number of low-cost destinations have opened up. Atlantic City, the gambling mecca, offers excursion fares from many cities with a two-day stay and no weekend requirement. Atlantic City is about 60 miles from Philadelphia and within striking distance of New York and Washington, DC.

Also on the East Coast, Baltimore's BWI is served by low-cost Southwest. Many other airlines have lowered fares to compete. If you're in Philly or Washington, you may want to check out the fares from Baltimore before choosing an airport closer to home.

Major metropolitan areas like New York and Los Angeles are served by many more airports than the ones that spring immediately to mind. For example, when most people think of New York airports, they think of Kennedy, LaGuardia, and Newark. But not too far away, you'll find Islip, White Plains, Bridgeport, Newburgh, even Philadelphia. Maybe there's a flight into or out of one of those airports that will offer a fare worth the extra time it takes you to travel to or from the less familiar airport. Of course, if you are flying in and picking up a rental car anyway, this might also offer an ideal opportunity to do some sight-seeing en route to your ultimate destination.

Here are some things to bear in mind:
- Fare differentials to various airports fluctuate up and down as rapidly as air fares themselves. Today's "hot" bargain may evaporate with changes in competition or other market factors.
- Figure in the cost and aggravation of driving when making your decision. Does it make sense to drive

100 miles to save $50? How about $150?

- Sometimes, a different airport will yield a savings only when combined with the split-ticket ploy.
- The existence of a fare differential to an alternate destination may indicate that your primary destination is a "hidden city" (see Ploy #13, below).
- Keep this ploy in mind when tickets to your primary destination are scarce for some reason (Super Bowl, World Series, the Olympics, etc.). You may not save big bucks, but at least you'll get a ticket.

Finding those airport alternatives

Figuring out whether a different airport will yield a lower fare will take some hunting around. A good travel agent can fire up the computer and do a quick search of the alternatives if you don't want to do the legwork yourself. Also, thanks to the industry grapevine, your travel agent will be up to date on which alternative routings offer the biggest savings.

For the dedicated do-it-yourselfer, here is a list of major airports, along with some nearby destinations that might not immediately spring to mind. Keep in mind that, while the fare to a lesser airport may be cheaper, the opposite may also be true. In other words, consider Hartford as an alternative to Boston and Boston as an alternative to Hartford. I have also listed the three-letter airport codes to help Internet users quickly compare published fares between your home and a number of different destinations. (I'll show you exactly how in Chapter Eight.)

Atlanta (ATL): Birmingham, AL (BHM); Chattanooga, TN (CHA)

Boston (BOS): Hartford, CT (BDL); Providence, RI (PVD)

Baltimore (BWI): Washington (Reagan) (DCA); Washington (Dulles) (IAD); Philadelphia, PA (PHL); Harrisburg, PA (HAR/MDT)

Southwest's entry into the Baltimore market has reduced fares dramatically.

Chicago (ORD/MDW): Milwaukee, WI (MKE); South Bend, IN (SBN)

In Chicago, Midway Airport (MDW) offers both close-in convenience and a higher probability of a lower fare than busy O'Hare (ORD).

Cincinnati, OH (CVG): Dayton, OH (DAY); Louisville, KY (SDF); Indianapolis, IN (IND)

Cleveland (CLE): Akron/Canton, OH (CAK); Toledo,
OH (TOL), Columbus, OH (CMH)

Columbus, OH (CMH): Dayton, OH (DAY); Akron/
Canton, OH (CAK); Cincinnati, OH (CVG)

Dallas/Ft. Worth (DFW): Austin, TX (AUS); Okla-
homa City, OK (OKC)

Detroit (DTW): Toledo, OH (TOL); Flint, MI (FNT);
Lansing, MI (LAN)

Denver (DEN): Colorado Springs, CO (COS)

Colorado Springs is not the great budget alternative it once was, but it is still worth keeping in mind, especially if low-fare competition is ever knocked out in the Denver market.

Houston (HOU, IAH): Austin, TX (AUS); San Anto-
nio, TX (SAT)

Los Angeles (LAX): Burbank, CA (BUR); Ontario,
CA (ONT); Long Beach, CA (LGB); Orange
County/Santa Ana, CA (SNA)

If you can stand the drive (and like to gamble), consider Las Vegas (LAS) as your gateway to southern California. Fares to the gambling mecca tend to be low thanks to some low-fare compe-tition and the steady stream of gamblers.

Miami (MIA): Fort Lauderdale, FL (FLL); West Palm
Beach, FL (PBI)

New Orleans (MSY): Baton Rouge, LA (BTR); Mo-
bile, AL (MOB)

New York/Newark (LGA, JFK/EWR): Islip, NY
(ISP), White Plains, NY (HPN), Newburgh, NY
(SWF), Atlantic City, NJ (ACY), Philadelphia (PHL)

When flying into New York City, your best bet for a low fare will be Newark (EWR). Taxi fares into the city are more expensive than they are from LaGuardia and JFK, but public transportation is easy and inexpensive. The Hudson River is a powerful psychological barrier in the region and seems to be the main reason for the fare differentials.

> **Orlando (MCO):** Tampa, FL (TPA); Sarasota, FL (SRQ); Daytona Beach, FL (DAB); Melbourne, FL (MLB); Jacksonville, FL (JAX)

Rental car rates tend to be lower in Florida, taking the sting out of driving to this vacation mecca from an outlying airport.

> **San Francisco (SFO):** Oakland, CA (OAK); San Jose, CA (SJC); Sacramento, CA (SMF)
>
> **Seattle (SEA):** Portland, OR (PDX)

There are many other possibilities, of course. A quick glance at a road map (or those airline route maps I urged you to start collecting) will suggest alternatives in other markets. Above all, remember that just because flying to Airport X isn't any cheaper this trip doesn't mean that flying there next time won't save you a bundle.

Ploy #9: Look for code-share bargains

Code-sharing is a reciprocal arrangement that lets an airline sell tickets to destinations served by another airline, thereby extending its marketing reach without a huge capital outlay. Under the typical code-share arrangement, each airline gets to sell seats on some of the other's flights just as if they were on their own airplanes. It's a great deal for the airlines but a questionable one for the flying public. For one thing, the airlines don't have to let you know when they are booking you on another carrier's plane for a portion of your journey. While they claim they will alert you, their track record on doing so is spotty. So if you have sworn for some reason that you will never, *never* fly on Airline X again, you may find yourself boarding one of its flights thanks to a code-share agreement with Airline Y.

This is not as unlikely a situation as you might think. Travel agents will tell you that there are many consumers who refuse to fly on anything but an American airline. Yet these same consumers can book overseas flights on a good old U.S. carrier and find themselves boarding a foreign flag carrier for the overseas portion of their trip.

Code-sharing is supposed to help the consumer by making

things easier. Code-shares can also help you build your frequent flyer miles, although just because two airlines are code-share partners does not necessarily mean their frequent flyer programs are linked. You'll have to check, but the airlines don't make it easy because they won't always tell you that you have just booked a code-share flight.

There are more serious problems. One is CRS bias. By law, the computerized reservations systems (CRS) owned by the airlines are not supposed to show bias by displaying one airline's flights more prominently than another's. Typically when a request is made to a CRS for flights between Point A and Point B, the system will display nonstop and direct flights first, on the theory that these are the most desirable. Next will be listed itineraries that require a change of plane on the same airline. Finally, the system lists so-called interline itineraries, those that require you to change planes from one airline to another. Code-sharing lets flights that used to be interline flights sneak up in the listings, thus increasing the chances that a travel agent will book them before even seeing possibly cheaper alternatives listed lower down (and a few computer screens away), definitely a concern to the budget-conscious traveler.

Of immediate interest to our current discussion is that code-sharing airlines do not always (in fact, seldom) price the same flights the same way. Industry observer Trippler has pointed out this phenomenon. He found a $534 price difference between New York-Warsaw fares offered by code-share partners American Airlines and LOT, the Polish national airline. Other differences he turned up: $105 between Houston and Toronto (United and Air Canada), $513 on a circle trip from Newark to Reno to Columbus to Newark (Continental and America West), and $994 on business class tickets between New York and Seoul (Delta and Korean Airlines). Here's one I stumbled across recently: To fly from New York to Amsterdam I could have paid TWA $1,203 or paid its code-share partner just $481. Remember now, regardless of which code-share partner you booked with in any of the above examples, you'd be flying on exactly the same airplane.

You can see a pattern here. The foreign partner in the code-share agreement usually has the lower fare. In the case of the Continental-America West code-share, America West has the reputation of being the low-fare carrier, although America West will not always be the cheaper alternative. I just checked a Phoenix-Fort Myers code-share routing and found Continental to be cheaper by $145! The challenge, then, is to find out which flights are code-share flights and check the pricing offered by both partners. Sometimes, an airline reservationist will be very upfront, other times you have to ask. *Always ask!* This is especially important if you are one of those people who are fussy about which airlines they fly.

If you are using the Internet as a research tool (see Chapter Eight), you should be able spot code-share flights by reading carefully and paying particular attention to the fine print. A recent random check of airline sites and online booking services showed that code-share flights were invariably identified and the name of the foreign flag carrier provided, although almost always in smaller type or in a footnote. Once you have identified a code-share flight, you can then price the foreign carrier's flight separately.

For most people, however, a savvy travel agent is probably the best bet for spotting and taking advantage of code-share situations. You can also check out those airline route maps I suggested you collect; oftentimes they will explicitly indicate which flight segments are operated by their code-share partners.

Here is a list of the code-share partners of major American airlines as they stood recently. However, things change and, as I write, the airlines seem to be falling all over themselves to forge new "alliances."

Alaska Airlines — Air China, American, Canadian Airlines, Continental, KLM, LanChile, Northwest, Qantas

America West — Air China, British Airways, Continental, EVA Air, Northwest

American Airlines — Aer Lingus, Aerolineas Argentinas, Air Pacific, Alaska, Asiana, Canadian Airlines, China Eastern, EVA Air, Finnair, Grupo TACA, Gulf Air, Hawaiian Airlines, Iberia, Japan Airlines,

LanChile, LOT Polish Airlines, Qantas, Sabena, Singapore Airlines, Swissair, TAM-Brazil, TAP Air Portugal

Continental Airlines — Air France, Alaska Airlines, Alitalia, America West, British Midland, COPA Airlines, CSA Czech, EVA Air, Hawaiian Airlines, Northwest, Virgin Atlantic

Delta Airlines — AeroMexico, Aeropostal, Air France, Air Jamaica, Air Portugal, China Southern Airlines, Malev, South African Airways, Transbrasil

Northwest Airlines — Air China, Alaska Airlines, America West, Big Sky, Continental, Continental Micronesia, Japan Air System, Eurowings, Hawaiian Airlines, KLM, Malaysia Airlines, Pacific Island Aviation

TWA — Air Malta, Kuwait Airways, Royal Air Maroc, Royal Jordanian

United Airlines — Aeromar, Aeromexico, Air Canada, Air New Zealand, ALM, Aloha Airlines, ANA, Ansett Australia, Austrian Airlines, British Midland, Cayman Airways, Continental Connections, Emirates, Gulfstream International, Lufthansa, Mexicana, SAS, Saudi Arabian Airlines, Singapore Airlines, SNCF, Spanair, Thai Airways, Trans States Airlines, Varig

US Airways — Air Midwest, Allegheny, CC Air, Chautauqua Airlines, Commute Air, Deutsche BA, Florida Gulf, Mesa, Mesa Liberty, Piedmont, PSA, Trans States Airlines

Of course, if you're traveling overseas, foreign airlines have their own code-share arrangements, such as the one between Singapore Airlines and Air India.

A final note

Just because you've found code-share partners offering radically different fares for the same flight don't automatically assume that you've found the cheapest way of getting to your destination. Other possibilities for a cheaper fare include low-fare airlines (see Chapter Four), consolidators (see Chapter Six), or even air courier flights (see Chapter Seven). The important thing is that, by being wise to code-shares, you will avoid the embarrassing possibility of overpaying for a flight you actually want to take.

Ploy #10: Buy roundtrip, fly one way

The time will come when you will be forced to fly one way. For example, you might have to fly to your parents' home and drive them back to yours in their car. Or maybe you're going somewhere with no idea of when (or from where) you will be returning.

Your first choice in a situation like this would be a low-fare airline (see Chapter Four). Their one way fares tend to be reasonable. However, if there is no low-fare carrier serving your destination you are likely to find that the one way fares on the major airlines are astronomical. (This in spite of their annoying way of advertising their cheap roundtrip fares as "one way based on roundtrip purchase.")

The solution is to purchase a roundtrip excursion fare and use only the outgoing coupon. You simply "miss" the return flight. If you are using this ploy, always make sure that the flight you want to take is the *first* coupon on the ticket. Otherwise, the airline will take note of your no-show status and cancel your return reservation. If you show up, ticket in hand, they will sock you for the full, last-minute, no-advance-purchase fare; they may also take the opportunity to make you feel like a criminal. For the same reason, it is a good idea to avoid giving your frequent flyer number when you decide to use this ploy.

Ploy #11: Buy one ways, fly roundtrip

If you are flying overseas in business class, ask your travel agent to see if it might be cheaper to buy two one way tickets instead of the usual roundtrip. This ploy works because the one way ticket for the return leg is, technically, being purchased abroad in the foreign currency. If exchange rates are working in your favor, you can sometimes realize significant savings. It is possible, but unlikely, that this ploy will work for leisure fares in coach class.

This is one ploy where you really need the assistance of a knowledgeable travel agent. If your travel agent has never heard of this way of purchasing tickets, it's time to look for another travel agent.

Ploy #12: Open jaw tickets

An "open jaw," in airline parlance, is a trip involving three cities, with no airline travel between two of them. Most frequently, a traveler will fly from home to one city and return from another. Occasionally, people will travel from one city, travel to another and then return from that city to a third city close to the original departure city. In any event, the line drawn on a map to illustrate such a trip resembles the open jaws of an alligator (or crocodile or whatever) and hence the name.

Occasionally, an open jaw trip will be cheaper than a standard roundtrip, but more often you are gaining flexibility, convenience, and time rather than saving money. Still, there are a number of reasons to consider an open jaw ticket.

If you are vacationing, an open jaw itinerary can let you see more. For example, you could fly into Orlando and back from Miami, or into San Francisco and back from Los Angeles. The same holds true when visiting Europe. I once used frequent flyer miles to fly into Amsterdam and back from Rome; it didn't cost me any additional miles and I didn't have to retrace my steps. If you have business dealings in Indianapolis, Cincinnati, and Louisville, why not visit all in one trip, flying into one and back from another, instead of making two or three separate trips?

The trick to open jaw tickets is finding an economical rental car deal between the two airports. In Florida, you should have no trouble finding a rental that will let you drop off at a different location at no extra charge. In other locations, you may have to shop around before finding such a deal. In some situations you may be forced to pay a "drop-off charge" of several hundred dollars, which might make you think twice about using an open jaw ticket.

To be a true open jaw trip, both legs must be on the same airline. Typically, the airline determines the open jaw fare by taking half the normal roundtrip fare between each city and adding the results. Otherwise you are purchasing two separate (and usually much more expensive) one way trips. Of course, if the two legs on your open jaw journey are on two different low-fare airlines (see Chapter Four), you may still be getting a bargain.

Ploy #13: Hidden cities

We now enter a shadowy area of ticketing ploys: ones that run contrary to the airlines' rules. It may come as a surprise to some readers that an airline ticket is not just another "product," but a contract between you and the airline. Every airline ticket is connected to something called the "Contract of Carriage," a lengthy compendium of rules of which you probably have never heard and certainly haven't read, but which you agree to abide by when flying with the airline in question. Most of the time, the rules don't matter much. However, the airlines' pricing strategies are so Byzantine that, increasingly, they offer sly and savvy travelers the opportunity to purchase tickets in such a way that they wind up paying less for a journey than the airline would like them to. In these cases, the airlines can get huffy.

It used to be that ticketing ploys that ran counter to airline rules were largely ignored. Perhaps the airlines tolerated a few sneaky travelers secure in the knowledge that most of the traveling public remained blissfully unaware of these money-saving ploys. But times change and the airlines began cracking down on these practices, usually by hitting the travel agents that issued the tickets with "debit memos," which recouped the income the airline would have received had the traveler paid the inflated price the airline wanted. Ironically, some airlines would let travelers use these "questionable" ticketing ploys when they booked directly with the airline (at least according to some reports in the travel trade press), but held travel agents to a higher standard. Now the airlines have taken the battle directly to the consumer, sending threatening letters to offenders (whom they catch through their frequent flyer numbers) and humiliating and threatening travelers they catch in the act.

One such tactic employed by business travelers seeking to avoid minimum stay requirements and outrageous one way fares is known as the "hidden city" ploy. Thanks to airline pricing structures, it is often less expensive to fly from City A to City B and catch a connecting flight to City C than it is to fly straight from A to B. City B is the "hidden city" in this equation. The canny business traveler purchases a ticket to the more distant city (City C), but deplanes when the plane lands at his actual destination (City B) and goes about his business. Here is an example:

A business traveler is facing yet another short midweek business trip, this time from Minneapolis to Detroit. The fare the airline wants him to pay for this quick roundtrip is $956 (or $478 each way, if purchased as two one way tickets). Instead, he buys two one way tickets as follows. Ticket one is from Minneapolis to South Bend, IN, requiring a change of planes in Detroit. This ticket costs $296, instead of $478. Ticket two is from Detroit to Peoria, IL, requiring a change of planes in Minneapolis. This ticket costs $184, instead of $478.

The total cost for both tickets is $480, a savings of $476 over the roundtrip fare. When he travels, he uses only the first coupon of each ticket and discards the second coupon.

The traveler is careful to book two separate tickets at two separate times, preferably with two different airlines. By doing this he keeps both the airlines and any travel agent he might be using in the dark about his intentions. If he's really smart, he won't add his frequent flyer number to either of these tickets. If airline annoyance with hidden city ticketing increases (and there is every indication it will), it would be a simple matter to crunch the numbers of frequent flyers searching for a pattern in which second coupons went unused.

Problems with hidden city tickets

The main problem with hidden city tickets is that the traveler can't check baggage. Any bags would be checked to the final destination and, of course, the traveler is not planning to go there. Some travelers report that they can tip the curbside check-in man to send the bags to the "hidden city" but this is courting discovery. Other travelers simply stick to carry-on luggage (an art that most business travelers have long since mastered) or over-night their luggage to their hotel. The savings on the ticket more than pay for the cost of overnight shipment in most cases.

The airlines don't like it when people turn their fare structures against them, and they are trying to catch them. That is why people who use this technique buy two separate tickets. If you bought, for example, a single ticket with four coupons reading Minneapolis - Detroit - South Bend - Detroit - Minneapolis, and planned only to use the first and fourth coupons, the airline's computer would alert counter personnel to the fact that you never used your coupons to and from South Bend. This could result in some unpleasantness when you tried to check in for the flight back to Minneapolis. In fact, you'd probably find your return trip had been cancelled.

For the same reason, savvy hidden city veterans always make the second coupon the unused one. If you bought a cheaper ticket from, say, Peoria to Detroit, with a change of plane in Minneapolis, discarded the first coupon, and then tried to board the flight in Minneapolis, the airline would know you were a "no show" in Peoria. They could ask you to prove that you actually flew from Peoria to Minneapolis. And that you wouldn't be able to do.

If you have a choice of three airlines to your "hidden city," determining which one will offer the best hidden city fare can take a bit of sleuthing. A good travel agent can help here. Just be aware of the tricky situation the travel agent is in vis-à-vis the airlines.

Is it "illegal"?

Good question. There is a school of thought that holds that how many coupons you use is your own darn business. There are no federal or state laws against it, but the fact is that no one knows whether this ploy is "legal" in the sense of "will it hold up in court?" The airlines' rules have yet to be challenged in court by someone caught using this ploy. There have been reports that the company of a business traveler who was caught using the hidden city ploy (and forced to pay up the difference) will challenge this in court. Let's wish them luck.

Of course, one way to make the hidden city ploy perfectly kosher in the eyes of the airline is to actually fly the second leg and use a rental car to return to the "hidden city." In this case, you are merely implementing the perfectly innocuous Ploy #7.

For me, however, the bottom line is this: All the major airlines have specific rules against hidden city ticketing. I cannot in good conscience recommend that you use this ploy. The only airline I know that doesn't specifically prohibit this type of ploy is Southwest, and that may change. And even so, given the current climate, I can't recommend using the ploy even then.

A so-called "Passengers' Bill of Rights" was introduced in Congress a couple of years ago. This legislation would have made it legal for travelers to use the hidden city ploy as well as back-to-back tickets (described below). With a flurry of publicity, the airlines responded by announcing that they were creating their own passenger bill of rights (which turned out to include mostly things they claimed to have been doing all along). Congress promptly killed the bill on the grounds that it was no longer necessary since they had brought the airlines to their knees with the mere threat of legislation. Your elected representatives thereby created the illusion of action without actually having to offend potential corporate campaign contributors. Not too surprisingly, the airlines' pledges have been honored more in the breach than the observance.

Ploy #14: Back-to-back ticketing

This is the mother of all "naughty" ticketing ploys, the one that gets most of the attention, the one that the airlines hate with a passion. And the one that probably leaves travelers most open to airline retaliation, unless they take extreme precautions, including foregoing frequent flyer miles when they use this ploy.

Back-to-back ticketing is a ploy used to save money when a planned trip does not include a Saturday night stay-over (and, hence, is not eligible for an excursion fare). In this case, the traveler buys two separate excursion tickets but uses only half of each ticket. Some examples, all using the same (unnamed) airline, will make this clearer.

The "classic" back-to-back ticket

Let's say you have to fly on business, from Chicago to Los Angeles, a few weeks from now, leaving on a Tuesday and returning the next Thursday. Your airline of choice is quoting a fare of $1,462 for this roundtrip. Yikes! But wait. The same airline is quoting a Chicago-LA roundtrip excursion fare of just $418. It doesn't take a Ph.D. in math to realize that two times $418 ($836) is a lot less than $1,462 — $626 less to be exact.

The solution: Buy two *separate* roundtrip excursion tickets. One leaves Chicago for LA on Tuesday and returns to Chicago on any date within a year after the Saturday following your departure. (Airlines typically restrict stays to less than a year.) The other ticket leaves LA for Chicago on the Thursday. The return coupon (Chicago to LA) can be for any date up to a year later. In the classic case, the business traveler simply uses the first coupon in each ticket and throws the second coupon away. A waste? Not really, the traveler has saved $626 on a trip that *had* to be taken.

The "twofer" back-to-back ticket

Of course, you don't *have* to throw away that second coupon. With a little planning you can use those second coupons, too. If you know you will be taking another business trip to LA within the next year, you can simply have the tickets written accordingly. For example, you could have the return date on the Chicago-LA-Chicago ticket be May 9 and the return date on the LA-Chicago-LA ticket read May 6. Now you would be able to fly from Chicago to LA on May 6 and return on May 9, using the second half of two different tickets. You could even write the tickets so you could spend an extended time (a vacation?) in LA later in the year.

Suppose you don't know when you might want to get back to LA? No problem. Book the tickets to give you the most leeway; that is, make the return date eleven to twelve months later on both tickets. When your schedule firms up, you can change the dates on the tickets. Doesn't that cost money? Of course it does, but only $50 or $75 for each ticket. Your second trip to LA costs you only $100 or $150!

Remember, on the first trip you fly from Chicago to LA on the first coupon of the first ticket; you return on the first coupon of the second ticket. On your second trip, you fly from Chicago to LA on the second coupon of the second ticket and return on the second coupon of the first ticket.

This ploy will appeal to business people who know they will have business reasons to be in a distant city more than once a year, but who don't want to take the time to stay over a Saturday to qualify for a lower fare. For example, do you have a key account in Dallas but just want to fly in and fly out? This ploy will give you two visits for less than the price of one.

It might also appeal to those who have put off short business trips because of the expense. If you knew you could get two short trips at a reasonable price, you might be convinced that the travel was worthwhile.

The "open jaw twofer"

A variation on the twofer concept lets you visit a *different* city later in the year. Let's say you don't need to get back to LA within the year, but you will have business in San Francisco. Or maybe you'd just like to go to San Francisco for a little vacation. In this case, you can take advantage of the airline's open jaw excursion fares.

An "open jaw" trip (described in Ploy #12) is one in which part of the journey (presumably) takes place over land. If you flew from Chicago to LA, rented a car and drove to San Francisco, then flew from San Francisco back to Chicago, that would be an open jaw trip.

When dealing with an excursion fare (those with a Saturday night stay), open jaw fares offer savings similar to those on straight roundtrip tickets. In the Chicago-LA example just cited, you could have booked tickets as follows: Ticket one would read Chicago-LA/San Francisco-Chicago. Ticket two would read LA-Chicago/Chicago-San Francisco. In this case, each ticket would cost $413 or $826 for both (as opposed to $1,462 for a Chicago-LA-Chicago roundtrip without a Saturday stay).

The first coupons of tickets one and two would be dated to

accomplish the business trip to Los Angeles. The second coupons would be given known dates for a second trip or given random dates far enough in the future to leave you a comfortable time in which to plan your future trip to San Francisco.

Open jaw twofers won't work for just any cities. Airline rules say that, for open jaw fare rules to apply, the open jaw (the "missing" part of the triangle) must be the shortest distance in the triangle. In other words, you couldn't start from Chicago and use this ploy to fly to LA first and then to a city like Miami or Washington, DC.

The "rock-bottom" back-to-back ticket

The "classic" back-to-back ploy is used by many business travelers because it is the simplest and most obvious; it offers demonstrable savings and it doesn't require much thought or research. However, if you know you are not going to be using the second coupons, there is a cheaper way to go, again taking advantage of open jaw fare pricing. You search for the open jaw city combo that will yield the lowest fare.

Let's say, once again, that you have to go from Chicago to LA for a few days. But you know that you will not be doing any other traveling to that part of the world during the next year. You could book your back-to-back ticket as follows: Ticket one reads Chicago-LA-Kansas City. Ticket two reads LA-Chicago (on the first coupon) and Kansas City-LA (on the second). You'd simply use the first coupon on each ticket and throw the second coupon away; you'd never see Kansas City.

Why Kansas City, you ask? Because it works. It meets the airline's open jaw rules and yields an ultra-low fare since the LA-KC legs are booked on a flight that stops in Dallas. Remember that the fare quoted to fly from Chicago to LA and return two days later was $1,462? In this example, the cost of each open jaw ticket is just $309 or two for $618. This represents a savings of $844, or $218 more than in the first example given above.

Obviously, it will take someone familiar with the ins and outs of airline fare structures to ferret out this precise configuration. Either that, or you will have to try out a number of combinations to find the one that works best. You can do this with an

OAG Travel Planner, on the Internet, or just by calling up the air-line reservations number a few different times and trying on different itineraries for size. Again, your best bet is to deal with a knowledgeable travel agent.

Problems with back-to-back tickets

The major problem with back-to-back tickets is that air-lines don't like them. Ticket prices are set up the way they are to stick it to the business traveler, and many airlines resent it when people figure out ways around them. All the major airlines now have explicit rules prohibiting the use of back-to-back tickets.

If they catch you, some airlines will deny you boarding, confiscate your ticket, and demand that you cough up the savings you realized by using this ploy. Some airlines are even incentivizing their counter personnel to detect back-to-back tickets. Travelers who have been caught report rude, threatening, and humiliating actions taken by the airlines.

Do the airlines have the right to do this? Well, some airlines obviously think so. Some industry observers, on the other hand, disagree. The fact is, the matter has never been tested in court. This, however, will be of little consolation should you find yourself stranded and humiliated at the airport. Unless you have a need to be a martyr or a test case, you should probably steer clear of back-to-back tickets.

The airlines can also make it sticky for the travel agent. In fact, since the airlines can "pull their plates" (i.e. make it impossible for the travel agent to sell their tickets), the travel agent is in a worse situation than the traveler. Nevertheless, many ornery travelers and their agents persist in using this family of ploys. Many report no problems. Here are some of the tactics they use:

- *Book with different airlines.* In many cases, it is possible to purchase each ticket from a different airline, thus vastly decreasing the odds of detection for the traveler. The travel agent, however, may not be reassured.
- *Book with different travel agents.* By booking each ticket with a different travel agent, the traveler solves the agent's tricky problem with the airlines. However,

it is uncertain whether the fact that the travel agent was an unwitting dupe would sway an airline bent on recovering money.

- **Book at different times with the same airline.** Travelers booking their back-to-back tickets on the same airline and having them mailed to them, will often do so at different times. If both tickets were booked at the same time, the reservationist would, presumably, immediately see what the traveler was doing. By booking the tickets at different times (even a few minutes apart), the theory is that the traveler will be dealing with different reservationists and the airline doesn't track things closely enough to pick up on the traveler's strategy. Presumably, a traveler could also book tickets at different times with the same travel agency; if the agency were busy enough and if the traveler dealt with a different agent on each occasion, the agency might not be aware of what was happening. Of course, this wouldn't help the agency much if the airline found out.

- **Be discreet when making changes.** When changing dates on the second coupon, veteran back-to-backers never present both coupons at the same time. Reason: Once again, the reservationist (or travel agent) would catch on to the ploy being used.

- **Keep tickets intact.** Seasoned back-to-backers don't mess with their tickets. If a traveler detaches and rearranges the coupons from the two tickets in the order he plans to use them, this is a sure tip-off to counter personnel at the airport. Veteran back-to-backers keep the two tickets separate and never produce more than one at the airport. They don't throw away any second coupons until they've used the first. In fact, no matter what your situation, you should never detach a coupon before the airline ticket-taker does so. The airlines are very fussy about the "integrity" of their tickets.

- **Don't use your frequent flyer number.** This just makes it easier for the airline to figure out what you're up to.

Another solution: The "not a back-to-back" ticket

This one really isn't a back-to-back ticket, but from the traveler's standpoint it looks and acts enough like a back-to-back ticket to be included here. It also has the advantage of not violating any airline rules.

Let's say a Boston-based business traveler has to fly from Boston to Dallas on a Monday and return on Wednesday. The fare is a whopping $1,236. But there's an alternative the airlines say is perfectly okay.

The trick is to book the trip as follows: First, a one way full-coach segment, followed by a roundtrip excursion fare. In other words fly from Boston to Dallas, one way in "Y" class (the airline code fare for full coach). Then fly from Dallas to Boston (and back to Dallas, presumably) on an advanced purchase excursion fare. Then simply don't use the last coupon (for the return flight to Dallas).

Book this as *one ticket* with three coupons and you've satisfied the airlines' picky rules. But you've paid just $963 for the ticket, including the unused portion — a savings of $273. You don't save as much using this ploy as you would with a "rock bottom" or even a "classic" back-to-back ploy, but you've broken no rules. Check with your travel agent to see if this ploy will work for you — and them — on a given itinerary.

Yet another solution: serial back-to-backs

This ploy will only work in special circumstances, but it has the virtue of providing most of the benefits of back-to-back ticketing without violating any airline rules.

Let's say you are a consultant and a project requires you to spend several days each week in another city. Rather than purchase a series of short-term, midweek roundtrips at an inflated price, consider this alternative: Purchase your first flight to the distant city as a one way ticket. Then purchase a series of roundtrip tickets *from the distant city* back home, each one bridging a weekend. That way you meet the Saturday-night-stay requirement for excursion pricing, and save a bundle in the process.

A final note on back-to-backs

Back-to-back ticketing is controversial and getting more so. The legality and enforceability of rules against back-to-back ticketing is a gray area at present. Critics of the rules make eloquent arguments against the restrictions. Eventually, some hearty traveler will take the airlines to court over this issue. Hopefully, he or she will win. Or perhaps the Airline Passengers' Bill of Rights, mentioned earlier, will be resurrected (it should be!) and make it through Congress. In the meantime, I cannot in good conscience recommend that you use this ploy.

Ploy #15: Right cities, wrong dates

An Atlanta-based consultant made frequent midweek trips to service a client in Ft. Lauderdale. In fact, she traveled so frequently that she enjoyed Platinum Medallion status in Delta's frequent flyer program, meaning she was in the top two or three percent of Delta flyers. Delta's "business" fare (i.e. no Saturday night stay) on this route was about $700; excursion fares, however, could be had for between $300 and $400. So she started maintaining a supply of cheap excursion-fare tickets. Also, if she held a valid ticket and her Ft. Lauderdale meeting was cancelled, she simply held on to the unused tickets.

On some occasions, when she needed to fly to Ft. Lauderdale on short notice, she would call Delta to book a flight at the $700 fare but at the gate present a ticket from her collection of unused or cheapie tickets. The hope was that the harried gate attendant wouldn't notice the dates weren't right. Occasionally, the consultant would be asked to pay a $75 change fee or would be assessed a fare difference, but most of the time no one noticed.

Until, that is, Delta's "Revenue Protection Unit" audited her frequent flyer account. They discovered that she had been very naughty between 20 or 30 times in a single year by using this ploy. Delta retaliated by dumping her from her Platinum Medallion status and docking her account 38,000 miles. Interestingly, they did not seek reimbursement for the fares the consultant *should* have paid.

Notice that the ploys discussed so far have involved buying perfectly valid tickets and then using them (or not using them) in creative ways. The Atlanta consultant, on the other hand, was knowingly presenting invalid tickets and, for many people (myself included) this ploy is a clear case of stepping over the line.

Now it can be argued that a certain amount of blame must lie with the gate attendants (perhaps that's why Delta didn't seek reimbursement), but it seems pretty clear to me that Delta had good reason to be annoyed.

I discuss this "ploy" not to encourage its use (I don't!), but because it illustrates some pertinent points:

First, the airlines are watching you and are willing to retaliate when they don't like what they see. My guess is that Delta's Revenue Protection Unit will be replicated at most of the major airlines. I further predict that we can look forward to the airlines becoming more, not less, aggressive in cracking down on *all* ticketing ploys they don't like. By going after an "elite" passenger, Delta was clearly sending a chilling message to the rest of us, just as the IRS likes to go after high-profile tax cheats.

Second, the reason Delta was able to nail the consultant in Atlanta was because she cheerfully provided them with her frequent flyer number every time she bought a ticket. When Delta confronted her, they were able to provide her with a spreadsheet that detailed her questionable flying activity.

So be forewarned: If you are going to do **anything** that the airlines might not like, regardless of how "legal" it might be or how unjustified you believe the airlines' rules to be, think twice about providing your frequent flyer number. Better yet, don't even *think* about providing your frequent flyer number.

Chapter Two

More Saving Ways

Chapter One concentrated (primarily) on ways to save money when purchasing tickets on the major domestic airlines by understanding, and capitalizing on, the ways in which their arcane ticketing rules work.

Now we turn our attention to other ways to shave dollars off your travel bill — by shopping in the right places, by taking advantage of discounts to which you may be entitled, even by profiting from the unpleasantness that from time to time mars the pleasures of travel.

Track sales and fare wars

I mentioned fare wars and fare sales briefly in Chapter One in connection with booking early. Of course, some sales require not only immediate action but almost immediate travel and will thus appeal mostly to the flexible traveler who can seize an opportunity when it presents itself or the lucky traveler whose travel schedule just happens to coincide with a fare war. Whatever your situation, keeping track of these great deals can prove problematical, but it's getting easier thanks largely to the Internet. Here are some tips:

- **Read the newspapers and watch TV.** Not only do airlines like to take out big ads announcing big sales but journalists have become eager PR flacks for the airlines when it comes to sales and fare wars. The fact that sales often mask or predict subsequent fare rises is seldom reported, but that's another story.

- *Subscribe to e-mail alerts.* Most airlines will now e-mail you bulletins on their weekly weekend fare sales as well as other special deals. It's also possible to subscribe to services that combine the fare news from a number of airlines. Chapter Eight has more information on how to do this.

- *More help from the 'Net.* Expedia's FareTracker system will send you weekly updates on the lowest fares to three destinations you specify. I have my Internet portal (the first screen I see when I fire up my browser) customized to show the lowest fare to five of my favorite destinations; when fares suddenly drop, I know something's up. See Chapter Eight for more.

- *Subscribe to* **Best Fares** *magazine.* The subscribers-only section of their web site (www.bestfares.com) lists short-fuse bargains, called "Snooze You Lose Fares." It's updated daily and can be addictive. The site also compiles weekly sales fares from the airlines in one convenient format.

Use a rebating travel agency

In recent years, the airlines have been steadily whittling away at the commissions they pay travel agents. One almost inevitable result is that many travel agencies have begun charging fees for issuing airline tickets. Amazingly enough, there are some agencies that will still give you back (rebate) a portion of the commission they receive when they issue your ticket.

How can they afford to do this? Well, for one thing they usually won't pay any rebate on very inexpensive tickets. When they do pay a rebate, it is fairly modest. Some of them tack on processing fees for mailing your tickets. Some require a membership or other upfront fee, making them rather like travel clubs, which are discussed later in this chapter.

There is no simple formula for using these agencies. In many cases, you will have to make the actual reservation yourself directly with the airline. You ask the airline to place your reservation on "courtesy hold" so you can pick up the ticket from your travel agent. Then you call the rebater, who will issue the ticket and send you a rebate check sometime later. Some of them have cumbersome paperwork requirements that an uncharitable observer might say are designed to discourage people from actually getting their rebate.

For me (and, I suspect, for many others), rebating travel agencies are more trouble than they're worth. The best time to use one is when you have to purchase a high-priced ticket (or several high-priced tickets) that you have already determined is the best deal you can get. For example, if you were faced with buying four international tickets with a base price of $1,400 on an airline paying a 10% commission, you might be able to get a rebate of as much as $245, which would probably be worth a few minutes of your time.

I would also encourage you to be leery of rebate offers on the Internet that require you to phone an 800 number and use a PIN number to book your travel. You are then instructed to e-mail the owner of the web site with your travel plans and are promised an unspecified rebate at an unspecified future date. It's not so much that these people are doing anything illegal or underhanded, it's just that they aren't offering much. These sites are set up by independent outside agents for so-called "referral travel agencies" (discussed in detail in Chapter Nine). Referral agencies offer their outside agents miniscule commissions on air fare, so there's not a lot to rebate. Also, the sites I've seen offer very few specifics on the details of their offer and no way (other than e-mail) to contact them in the event of a dispute. Of course, if you are booking a high-ticket cruise or tour through the agency, the rebate might actually be worth something.

Some rebaters

What follows is a partial list of rebating travel agencies. There are probably more; but my guess is that, with the airlines chipping away so assiduously at the travel agency community, they won't last long.

Best Fares magazine
(800) 880-1234
www.bestfares.com
Among the bells and whistles attached to a subscription to this monthly consumer magazine is membership in The Instant Rebate Club. Rebates range from 4% for tickets $350 and over to 5% on packages booked through airline tour departments. The most you can get back on a domestic ticket is $25; there is no maximum on an international ticket. Vacation packages must be reserved with the airline first, but airline tickets can be booked directly with the magazine's travel club (see below). See Chapter Ten for more on *Best Fares* and how to subscribe.

ISE Flights
(800) 255-7000
www.isecard.com
Obtaining a rebate on tickets over $150 from ISE Flights requires purchasing an "International Student Exchange" card that costs $25 a year. To qualify, you must be under 26 years of age, or a student, or a faculty member. ISE calls your school to verify the latter two. You are required to make your reservation with the airline first, asking them to put the reservation on "courtesy hold" and give you the "record locator number." Then you call ISE with the price and the number. They will rebate $10 on a domestic ticket and $50 on an international ticket. Any destination within North America (U.S., Canada, or Mexico) is considered domestic.) The rebate check is mailed with the ticket. Reservations made through travel agents or on the web cannot be processed.

Travel Avenue
(800) 333-3335
www.travelavenue.com
This Chicago travel agency bills itself as the country's oldest rebating travel agency. They promise to find the lowest fare and then provide either a rebate or an even

lower net fare. For domestic travel, they offer a $10 rebate on published fares over $350 and a $20 rebate on fares over $625. For international travel, they will quote both the best published fare minus a 5% to 12% rebate (depending on the airline) plus a $25 processing fee, and a lower consolidator fare, letting you choose which alternative you prefer.

The special case of TWA

TWA has had a turbulent relationship with its former CEO and chairman, corporate raider Carl Icahn. To some, he is evil incarnate for his perceived role in nearly destroying a once proud airline; to others, he is simply American business as usual. Whatever your opinion of Mr. Icahn, one salient fact concerns us here: In 1995, as part of a repayment deal for a 1992 loan, Icahn pocketed a cool $615 million. Not in coin of the realm but in TWA airline tickets.

Since not even Carl Icahn is *that* frequent a flyer, he is now selling off those tickets at a discount through a company called Global Discount Travel Services and its Internet affiliate, Lowestfare.com, both located in Las Vegas, NV. The toll-free numbers are (800) 497-6678 and (888) 333-0440. You can also book directly on the Internet at www.lowestfare.com.

The typical discount seems to be 20% on TWA flights. Lowestfare.com also offers a wide range of other discount flights. Global Discount Travel is not the only outlet for these tickets and many discount travel agencies offer the same tickets at similar discounts. It shouldn't be too difficult to find an agency near you that is ready, willing, and able to deal in these tickets.

Buy overseas

Leisure travelers venturing abroad should look into the possibility of dividing their air ticket purchases between the U.S. and overseas. Thriving markets in discounted tickets exist in a number of major foreign destinations, London, Frankfurt, Hong Kong, Singapore, and Bangkok among them.

For example, you could fly to London on a cheap fare and

then shop London's "bucket shops" for a cheap fare to one of the warm weather destinations— like Cyprus or Mauritius — popular with British holidaygoers. The combined fares can still be cheaper than arranging a direct flight, plus you get to savor the pleasures of London en route!

Here's another possibility: you want to explore Myanmar and Laos, but instead of making all the arrangements in the United States, you shop for a cheap flight to Bangkok (not too hard to find) and use a local travel agent to handle the visa hassles and arrange cheap flights. Not only are you taking advantage of one of the world's most active air fare bazaars but you will be dealing with travel agents well versed in dealing with the bureaucratic twists and turns of these reclusive countries.

Typically, you will get your best deal by waiting until you arrive, although you run the risk of either discovering nothing to your liking or, worse, that your trip will cost more not less. You can, of course, make arrangements from home. Phone and fax communication is easier and the costs cheaper than they have ever been in the past.

So, how do you find out about these off-shore sources? In addition to my book, *Air Travel's Bargain Basement: The International Directory of Consolidators, Bucket Shops and Other Sources of Cheap Travel*, you can find listings of discount travel agencies in foreign magazines like London's *Time Out*, which are increasingly available on the vast magazine stands in the book superstores. The Lonely Planet series of guidebooks is an excellent source of intelligence on discount travel agents in cities around the world.

Grow old

Age hath its privileges, and among them is a discount on air travel. If you are at least 62 years old (there are a few exceptions), the major airlines will extend a 10% discount on their published fares. The discount may not be available in some circumstances, but it seems pretty universal. If you are 62, you should always ask for it. Many airlines will extend the discount to a companion of any age traveling with the senior. In addition, some airlines have special senior fares available to selected destinations; typically these are companion fares, requiring that two people travel together. Low-fare airlines (see Chapter Four) are less likely to extend senior discounts, but it's worth asking. Whenever you fly on a senior discount, make sure you have not only the usual proof of age documentation, but any special airline membership cards that might be required as well.

Some of the major airlines also offer membership programs, and all of them will sell coupon books to seniors.

Senior membership programs

Each program differs, but typically your paid membership entitles you to discounted travel during your membership period. Some programs offer a flat discount of 15% to 20% off the regular fare, while others let you purchase coupons that can then be exchanged for fixed fares. These are determined either by a zone system or by mileage between cities. Most memberships come with additional savings coupons, frequent flyer bonuses, and other goodies.

Picking the right deal for you will require careful shopping. Obviously, if you live in or near an airline hub city, that airline's program will be most attractive to you. Check, too, to see which destinations are available; this is where route maps will come in handy. Be sure to check on maximum length of stay restrictions and blackout dates before signing up. Most important, don't assume that the fare available through a senior club program is invariably the best. Often better deals can be found elsewhere or by taking advantage of special sales and promotions.

The more travel time you have (in other words, the more retired you are), the more these programs will make sense. Check out the clubs listed on the following pages, request information from those that make the most sense, then take out the magnifying glass (you're a senior, remember) and read the fine print.

Senior coupon books

All of the major airlines offer coupon books, typically containing four coupons, each valid for a one way trip. The per coupon cost is typically somewhere between $130 and $150, and some trips require using more than one coupon. So, once again, these deals may not always be the best available at any given time; always check promotional and sales fares as well as low-fare alternatives before using a senior coupon. Some airlines allow coupons to be used for a younger companion traveling with you, others offer companion coupon books priced somewhat higher. Seats allocated to senior coupons are capacity controlled, which means that booking as early as possible is a good idea. Typically, coupons must be used within a year of purchase; however, you can use a coupon on the last day of eligibility to buy a ticket for a trip that won't occur until a year later.

The best time to use a senior coupon is when you have to travel on short notice, since most airlines allow them to be used on a standby basis. They can also come in handy when you want to go somewhere for an extended period of time and the cheap published fares have too-short maximum stay requirements.

Airline senior discount offerings

What follows is a list of the major airline senior programs, along with some notes on their current offerings. In most cases, the toll-free number given is specific to their senior program and is not a general reservations number. Since programs and pricing change periodically, it's always a good idea to check for the latest; the airlines will be happy to send you complete information. Also, this listing is not intended to be exhaustive. If an airline that is not listed serves your market, it might be a good idea to give them a call and see what they are offering seniors.

The fares quoted do not include the seemingly ever-growing list of taxes, passenger facility charges (PFCs), segment fees, departure taxes (in Hawaii and Puerto Rico), customs fees (in Canada), and on and on and on. To find the correct web page for an airline's senior program, log onto the main site, then click through the headings provided in the listings.

America West
(800) 235-9292
www.americawest.com (Products & Services, Products, Seniors)
Four coupons cost $548 ($137 each); 14-day advance purchase required. There are also blackout dates.

American Airlines

(800) 237-7981

www.americanairlines.com (Specials, Senior Fares)
American offers a 10% fare discount to seniors 62 and up and one companion on most flights. Seniors can also join the AActive American Traveler Club for $45 ($75 for a companion of any age). This program entitles the member to reduced fares anywhere American flies; fares are based on a zone system and travel on Fridays, Saturdays, and Sundays is not allowed. A separate program lets seniors purchase Senior TrAAveler Coupon Booklets. Four coupons cost $596 ($149) and a coupon can be redemmed for a one way coach flight in the U.S., Puerto Rico or the U.S. Virgin Islands. Two coupons are required for one way travel to Alaska and Hawaii. A 14-day advance purchase is required, but there are no blackout dates.

Continental Airlines

(800) 441-1135

www.continental.com (Search for Freedom Flight Club)
The Freedom Flight Club is open to those 62 and over for $75 a year ($125 if you want to travel outside the U.S.). Domestic discounts are 20% for travel Monday through Thursday and Saturday, 15% Friday and Sunday. To Europe, Saturday is also a 15% discount day. Continental's four-coupon books cost $579 ($144.75), but they also offer an eight-coupon option for $1,079 ($134.88). Mexico, Canada, and the Caribbean are included in this deal, but trips to Alaska and Hawaii require two coupons. A 14-day advance purchase is required and blackout dates apply.

Delta Airlines

(800) 325-3750

www.delta-air.com/SkyWise
Delta's SkyWise program has reached its membership limit and enrollment for the 2000-2001 program is closed. However, you can call to have your name placed on the waiting list.

Midway Airlines
(800) 446-4392

www.midwayair.com/special.html

You only have to be 60 to purchase four coupons for $390 ($97.50); companion coupon books are $440 ($110). If you can fly out of Midway's Raleigh/Durham, NC, hub the prices are even lower, $350 ($87.50) and $385 ($96.25) respectively. All flights require a 14-day advance purchase.

Northwest Airlines
(800) 692-6961

NorthBest Senior Travel Coupons are four for $596 ($149) and are good for travel in all 50 states and Canada. Longer trips may require up to three coupons. There are no blackout dates for using them.

Southwest Airlines
(800) 435-9792

www.southwest.com/traveler-info/seniors.html

The low-fare leader offers even lower senior fares to those 65 or older. This discount is not available to any companions traveling with the senior.

United Airlines
(800) 720-1765

www.silverwingsplus.com

United's Silver Wings Plus program is open to everyone over 55, which sets it apart. It also offers a lifetime membership option for $225, a real bargain if you plan to hang around awhile. If you're hedging your bets, the cost is $75 for a two-year membership. The program rules are more complicated than some and promotions change frequently. A typical promotion entitles you to purchase coupons (recently, $25 for four) which are redeemed for special low fares to U.S. destinations. Fares are based on roundtrip mileage between cities and recently ranged from $98 for a roundtrip of under 500 miles to $798 for one of over 9,000 miles, with weekend travel costing $30 more. Membership also includes dollars-off certificates.

United's Silver TravelPac coupon books, available to those over 62, are priced at four for $541 ($135.25). Savings certificates you receive when enrolling in the Silver Wings Plus program can be applied toward these coupons.This is a separate program, however, with a separate phone number, (800) 633-6563.

US Airways
(800) 428-4322

www.usairways.com/reservations/services.htm

Golden Opportunities coupon books are four for $579 ($144.75) and are good in the U.S., Canada, Mexico, Puerto Rico, and the Virgin Islands.You can also use them for grandchildren ages two through 11.

Stay young

The student and youth population has not inspired the same proliferation of discounts and offers from the airline community as have their grandparents. For one thing, much student travel is non-discretionary — to school in September and home for the holidays. These are high-demand travel periods and the airlines are not about to get generous then. And besides, Mom and Dad are often willing to pay an inflated price to see their little darlings.

Student leisure travel is discretionary, time-limited and predictable — Europe in the summer, south at Spring Break. For these reasons, the market has long been served by student travel specialists who use consolidator and tour operator techniques, charters, and group buying through student membership organizations to address the market.

Nonetheless, discount programs targeted at the younger crowd do crop up from time to time and they are worth knowing about if you qualify. Here are some of them. Be aware that these programs have a tendency to come and go, so some of these may be past history and others may have come into existence by the time you read this.

AirTran
(888) 493-2737

www.airtran.com

The "X-Fares" program lets young adults (18 through 22) fly on a standby basis for $47 (plus passenger facility charges or PFCs) per segment. You have to show up at the airport on the day of travel to get on the standby list (first-come, first-served). If there's an empty seat after the last boarding call, it's yours. X-Fares are not available on Fridays and Sundays and, if past experience is anything to go by, during the last half of December and early January.

American Airlines

(800) 433-7300

www.aa.com

American's College SAAver program requires signing up at its web site for periodic e-mail alerts about special offers for the college crowd.

Delta Airlines

(800) 221-1212

www.delta-air.com

On shuttle service between Boston, New York, and Washington, Delta offers a substantial discount ($90 versus $202 one way) to those ages 12 to 24. It also offers the Delta Shuttle Flight Pack, four coupons for $232 ($58 per flight) or eight for $413 ($52.63). The catch is, you must travel between 10:30 am and 2:30 p.m. or after 7:30 p.m. on weekdays; Saturday and Sunday you can travel all day.

Midwest Express

(800) 452-2022

www.midwestexpress.com

Midwest has student fares "available on select routes to students age 17-26 with a valid college or university ID."

TWA

(800) 221-2000

www.twa.com

TWA sells a four-coupon Youth Travel Pak for $548 ($137 per flight) to students 14 through 24. The coupons are good on domestic flights and a few destinations in Canada and the Caribbean. Trips to Hawaii require two coupons in each direction. Each Youth Travel Pak comes with a certificate good for a 20% discount on a European ticket.

Fly space available

It might make sense that you could go to the airport and pick up an unsold seat on a soon-to-depart plane for a bargain price. Unfortunately, it doesn't work that way. Some airlines let you standby for an earlier flight if you already hold a ticket to the destination, but that doesn't save you money, just time. A few international airlines — Virgin and Icelandic among them — have been known to announce last-minute fare sales on flights with a critical mass of empty seats (to coin an oxymoron), but in general getting a bargain by waiting until the very last minute works better for tours and cruises than for airline seats.

An exception to this rule is space-available travel, aimed largely but not exclusively at the student market. This travel strategy requires a high degree of flexibility and a high tolerance for inconvenience. The primary destination is Europe, although space-available companies also offer trips to the Caribbean and Hawaii. Here's how it works:

You register with a space available specialist and agree to fly from a "region" in the U.S. to a "region" in Europe during a "window" of from one to five days. You only learn which flights are actually available about a week before departure. The catch is that you may live in New York and be offered a flight from Boston or Washington. You may want to fly to Frankfurt but be offered a choice of Madrid, Paris or Copenhagen. Most space-available companies treat Europe as one large "region" so the inconvenience factor can be considerable. You do have the option of waiting for your "ideal" routing to materialize, but that courts the risk of blowing your whole vacation. Typically, flights are sold on a one way basis, so you must repeat the process, with all its attendant uncertainty, on the return leg.

The good news is that the one way fares are cheap, from

roughly $169 from the east coast to $249 from the west coast. The bad news is that sometimes people get stranded in Europe, especially when they are trying to return at the end of August or the beginning of September. If your Eurail Pass has expired and you suddenly have to get from Madrid to Berlin, or if you absolutely positively must return by a date certain and are forced to buy a high-priced return ticket, your savings can evaporate quickly.

This scheme works best for those who have purchased a Eurail Pass and just want to bop around Europe for an extended period of time. It's probably not a great strategy for someone who has her heart set on a week in Paris.

Here are two companies that specialize in this low-cost, high-risk travel option. Both of them also offer roundtrip flights to the Caribbean for about $250 and one way flights to Hawaii from the west coast for about $129. Both of them maintain web sites that explain their policies and procedures in great detail. I would recommend studying them carefully before doing anything rash.

Airhitch
2641 Broadway, Suite 100
New York, NY 10025
(800) 326-2009
(212) 864-2000
or
13470 Washington Boulevard, Suite 205
Marina del Rey, CA 90292
(888) 247-4482
(310) 574-0090
www.airhitch.org

Air-Tech Ltd.
588 Broadway
Suite 204
New York, NY 10012
(212) 219-7000, ext. 206
www.airtech.com

Get bumped

Sometimes airlines overbook a flight, that is they sell more tickets than there are seats on the plane. Why? Because bitter experience has shown them that not everyone who books a flight shows up for it, resulting in empty seats and lost revenues. Truth be told, with the continuing sophistication of computers and their programmers, the airlines are doing a better job of guessing right than they once did, but overbooking continues to be a problem. When this happens people have to be "bumped" or removed from the flight, voluntarily if possible, involuntarily if necessary.

If you absolutely, positively have to get where you're going being bumped can be a royal pain in the neck. You can reduce the possibility of involuntary bumping by getting an advance seat assignment and arriving for your flight early and getting to the gate promptly. If you show up at the last minute for an overbooked flight, chances are you will have already been involuntarily bumped and the airline will owe you nothing. On the other hand, if your travel plans are flexible or if you'd just as soon have an excuse for spending a little less time hearing Mom remind you what a disappointment you are to the family, getting bumped can be a positively wonderful experience, especially since it can put extra travel dollars in your pocket. Here's how it works.

If the airline is forced to bump people involuntarily, government rules require it to pay off the bumped passengers in cold hard cash. Voluntarily bumped passengers, however, can be compensated in vouchers redeemable for future flights (a better deal in my humble opinion). The voucher might be for a roundtrip flight or a specific dollar amount that can be used much like cash. Finding volunteers is far preferable for the airline because it is cheaper and better PR. So if a flight is overbooked, the airline wants to find volunteers.

If a flight is overbooked and you wouldn't mind being bumped, you have two choices. Volunteer immediately and grab what you can get or hope that the airline can't find enough volunteers and will sweeten the pot. The downside of the second alternative is that you may wait too long and wind up taking the flight. On the other hand, there may be occasions in which you initially don't want to be bumped but the compensation offered becomes irresistible. This happened to my wife and me on an American flight from the Caribbean; when the bidding got up to $700, we decided what the heck and volunteered for bumping. (American has a reputation for being especially generous in this regard, which probably explains why they have the lowest involuntary bumping stats in the industry.) As it turned out, we reached New York ahead of everyone else because the later flight on which we were booked was a non-stop.

If you volunteer immediately, ask what the compensation will be, and don't hesitate to negotiate a better deal. Whether you volunteer immediately or later, there are some additional guidelines to follow:

- Ask on which flight you will be rebooked.
- Request a meal voucher if the delay will be longer than a few hours. You might also request additional benefits such as use of the airline's club lounge.
- An alternative to being bumped (and just as good for some people) is volunteering to be upgraded to business or first class.
- If you discover that being bumped will result in more inconvenience than was immediately apparent, ask for increased compensation.
- If you are forced to stay overnight and the airline doesn't pick up your hotel tab (you should request they do), explain to the airport hotel that you've been bumped and ask for their "distressed passenger rate." It can be a real money-saver.

If you are actively looking to get bumped, arrive at the gate early and inquire about the booking status of the flight. If it is overbooked or close to being full, signal your willingness to be bumped which will get you a position at the top of the "bump list." The most likely dates to be bumped are the day before Thanksgiving and the Sunday after. The same is true of the few days before Christmas and New Year's Day and the few days after. Friday and Sunday afternoons and evenings are also likely to have overbooked flights on popular routes. Overbooking is otherwise unpredictable and can often be caused by bad weather or equipment problems, when cancelled flights cause overbookings on later flights, often in airports far from the original cause of the problem.

Once you have your voucher, you generally have one year in which to use it or lose it. Some airlines will let you extend the validity period for a month or two if you ask in sufficient time. Remember, too, that you can use your voucher on the last day of validity to purchase a ticket for a trip that is a year away. If you cash in some of the voucher, the money left over will go into a new voucher, which will usually have a new expiration date a year hence.

Complain with class

Getting bumped may be the most aggravating thing that can go wrong with an airline journey but, as I'm sure you know, there are a lot of others. Sometimes they are the sort of things you sigh and shrug off. Sometimes they are the sort of things that have you screaming mad and firing off nasty letters to the FAA, the DOT, your congressional representative, and the president of the airline. In the latter case, don't be surprised if the airline tries to mollify you (buy you off, some would say) with a voucher for future travel. Sometimes you will even be handed a voucher (typically a small one) by a flight attendant on the plane if you're really upset and seem to have a genuine beef. Given these precedents, it makes sense that if you have a valid complaint you deserve appropriate compensation.

Please understand that I am not suggesting that you make a habit or hobby of complaining to the airlines and I am certainly not encouraging you to manufacture excuses to complain. But, if you have a valid complaint why not turn it to your advantage? For your convenience, I have posted a list of airline complaint departments at www.BeatTheAirlines.com/complaints.html

There is an art to complaining. Crude and brutish attempts to intimidate the airline with threats of legal action are (I hope) beneath you — no matter how effective they may be. Understand that by bringing an unpleasant situation to the airline's attention you are providing them with an opportunity to take steps to avoid a recurrence. You are in fact doing them a favor. After all, no airline *wants* to annoy its passengers, no matter what the appearances. So draft your complaint letter in a calm and dignified manner, providing the airline with complete details of date, time, flight number, the names of airline personnel involved, and so forth. Clearly set forth the cost of the incident to you, in time, money, inconvenience, and aggravation. Finally, take the additional step of suggesting what you consider to be fair compensation for your suffering and inconvenience. Suggest that if you receive what you request, you will consider your grievance resolved, but reserve the right to file a formal complaint and send a copy of the letter to the Aviation Consumer Protection Division, Department of Transportation, C-75, 400 7th Street SW, Washington, DC 20590. The phone number is (202) 366-2220 and the web site is www.dotgov/ost/ogc/org/aviation/index.html.

The similarly named Aviation Consumer Action Project, 529 14th Street NW, Suite 1265, Washington DC 20045, (202) 638-4000, is one of consumer fanatic Ralph Nader's organizations. They can provide information, guidance, and a shoulder to cry on. The web site is www.acap1971.org.

Finally, if you're just plain mad, you might want to post your complaint on the Internet at eComplaints (www.ecomplaints. com). They forward all complaints to the airlines, but don't hold your breath. They tell me some airlines do respond, but a random check of complaints filed in the first half of 1999 revealed not a single airline response.

Join a travel club

Travel clubs are like food co-ops. A group of consumers band together and use their combined buying power to buy in bulk at a lower unit cost. Unlike food co-ops, travel clubs are slick operations run for profit by people who expect to make a good living. But the principle remains the same. By paying your fee to join the travel club, you are looking to receive sufficient discounts over the next year (the typical membership period) to recoup your membership fee and then some. Obviously, then, the more you travel, the more attractive these deals will be.

Most travel clubs cover far more than air fare, and you are likely to realize most of your savings from other travel products, especially cruises and tours where the discounts can be especially attractive. Discounts on air fare tend to take the form of a typically modest rebate and may require inconvenient paperwork and procedures.

Some travel clubs offer airline coupons, typically as a sort of sign-up bonus. These tend to be heavily restricted but if you use them, they can recoup the membership fee and then some almost immediately. Getting the most out of a travel club means finding the one whose offerings most closely mesh with your travel tastes and needs and then making a commitment to use your club benefits as often as possible.

There are some highly questionable offers, even scams, masquerading as travel clubs. If the cost of membership quoted by a travel club is many hundreds or even thousands of dollars, walk away from it. Legitimate travel clubs usually charge a reasonable rate. I would think long and hard about joining any club that charged more than $50 or $60 a year. Make sure to read the fine print in the materials you receive from any travel club. If anything is unclear, ask questions and make sure they are answered to your satisfaction. If possible, get a recommendation from someone who has used a particular travel club and found it a good value for the kind of travel you do.

Ambassadair Travel Club

(800) 225-9919

www.ambassadair.com

This outfit claims to be the nation's largest travel club. It is affiliated with American Trans Air (ATA), on which members receive a 10% discount; so it will be most attractive if you live in Chicago or Indianapolis (ATA's two hubs). All the other flights available are charters organized by the club. Membership is a hefty $149 per person or $199 for a family, with $99 yearly dues for both types of membership thereafter.

Best Fares **Magazine**
(800) 880-1234
www.bestfares.com
A $60 annual subscription to the magazine includes automatic enrollment in their travel club. The airline benefits were described above. Discounts on hotels, cars, cruises, and tours are also offered.

The Travel Club
(800) 292-9892
www.1800airfare.com
Annual dues are $49.95 ($94 for couples) and children under 12 traveling with their parents are eligible for full club benefits. Airfare rebates on published fares click in on tickets over $100 and are 4%, to a maximum rebate of $25. They also offer discounted fares that are not subject to rebate. The club has its own frequent flyer program that earns you "points" for all airline travel booked through the club.

Travel Holiday Gold Club
(877) 465-3167
www.travelholiday.com
Travel Holiday magazine has taken over the National Travel Club, the country's oldest. The annual membership fee of $29.97 ($19 for associates) includes a subscription to the magazine as well as the services of a 24-hour travel agency offering discounts on air fares, car rentals, and vacation packages. The club also offers 50% off regular rates at 2,300 hotels, discounts of up to 25% on books from major travel publishers, and up to $50,000 of travel insurance for the first year, with an option to renew.

Travel Portfolio
(800) 331-8867
www.memberweb.com
Annual dues are $49.95 with a "spouse card" $15 more. They offer air ticket rebates of up to 5% as well as discounted air fares.

Traveler's Advantage

(800) 548-1116

www.travelersadvantage.com

The main attraction here is 50% off selected hotels and 30% off most car rentals, along with special deals on cruises. On air fares, they make a "Low Price" claim for 424 airlines and offer 5% cash back on top of that. Getting the rebate requires sending in your receipts and itinerary. They usually offer an introductory three-month membership for $1 and throw in a free hotel night and some airline discount coupons. After that, annual membership is $60 a year.

Use dollars-off coupons

Adding a sweetener or a premium to encourage customers to part with their money is a well-known retail ploy. And what better come-on than a big discount on an airline ticket? Air fare discounts in consumer promotions are more prevalent than you might imagine.

Discount amounts can be $25, $50, $100, or more depending on the price of the ticket against which you apply the coupon. Some promotions take the form of certificates good for a specific fare on specific routes. You can find these coupons attached to all sorts of merchandise, but perennial favorites of the marketers seem to be supermarkets and videocassettes. In the case of supermarkets, you will typically receive one coupon for every $50 or $100 you spend on "qualifying purchases." With the videos, coupons are typically used to goose up sales of specific titles. Buying a $15 or $20 video to save $100 on a flight you want to take makes sense even if you don't like the movie — you can always give it as a gift to a despised in-law.

The problem with these offers is remembering to be on the lookout for them as you go about your shopping chores. If your local supermarket runs one of these promotions, it will probably be well advertised, but you may miss the promo being run at the market a few miles away, or the coupons tucked in with the razor blades or kiddie videos.

For the inveterate bargain hound, the perfect solution is a

subscription to *Best Fares* Magazine (see Chapter Ten again), which makes something of a fetish of tracking promotions such as these.

Chapter Three

Frequent Flyer Miles

Frequent flyer miles are a drug. A soft drug, perhaps, a recreational drug most definitely, but a drug nonetheless. Like any drug they can make you feel good and cloud your judgment at the same time.

Frequent flyer programs, which give passengers points for miles flown and then award "free" travel in exchange for these points, were created by the airlines to promote customer loyalty. They have been extremely successful in attaining this goal, so much so that many people make travel decisions to gain frequent flyer miles with little regard for the financial consequences.

Business travelers are notorious for this kind of thing, perhaps because the person doing the actual traveling isn't paying for the ticket. They'll choose a major airline over a low-fare airline, despite a fare difference of hundreds of dollars. Or they'll pick a more expensive flight or routing simply because they are closer to a travel award on the airline operating the more expensive alternative. The people who run corporate travel departments, and who are responsible for holding travel expenses in check, lose sleep (not to mention hair) because of this sort of thing.

When someone else is picking up the tab, it may be easy to understand this kind of behavior. Harder to fathom are the many travelers shelling out their own hard-earned money who will choose a more expensive flight simply because it offers frequent flyer miles. Does this make any sense? Seldom, if ever.

According to *Consumer Reports Travel Letter* the redemption value of a single frequent flyer mile is between one and two cents, sometimes a bit more depending on how wisely you "spend" it. So let's say you're going to Europe and you have a choice between a $300 discount ticket with no frequent flyer miles and a $500 ticket that gives you 7,000 frequent flyer miles. If you choose the latter, you will pay nearly 2.86 cents for each of those one or two cent frequent flyer miles ($200 divided by 7,000). When you cash those miles in, they will buy you $70 to $140 worth of ticket, probably closer to $70. The $200 you would save by buying the cheaper ticket, however, will buy you a full $200 worth of ticket. If, however, the cheapest ticket without frequent flyer miles is $430, you can justify buying the $500 ticket.

Let's take a domestic example of a short one way flight that earns 500 frequent flyer miles on a major airline. But let's say there's a low-fare airline on the same route. The fare difference would have to be less than $5 before opting for the major airline would make financial sense. Actually, the low-fare airline might have its own frequent flyer program, one that requires just twelve one way segments to qualify for a free roundtrip. So your frequent flyer credit on the low-fare carrier is the equivalent of one twelfth of a roundtrip ticket. If a roundtrip is worth $179, you've got $14.91 in invisible play money compared to the $5 to $10 you'd have by flying the more expensive major airline.

If you have sufficient frequent flyer miles to splurge on a business or first class ticket, the equation becomes favorable. In fact, a frequent flyer mile spent for a business class ticket can be worth seven cents or so.

However, most of us aren't sitting on huge piles of frequent flyer miles, so when making this type of calculation, I would encourage you always to use one cent as the market value of each frequent flyer mile. If you flatter yourself that you'll always get at least two cents per mile when you cash them in, you'll most likely be deluding yourself. At one cent a mile, you have a good chance of coming out ahead in the long run.

The moral of the story is simple: Ignore frequent flyer miles; always seek out and buy the cheapest ticket. The only exception is when the price difference divided by the number of frequent flyer miles at stake is .01 or less (an unlikely occurrence), or when someone else is paying for the ticket and doesn't seem to care that you are putting your own selfish interests ahead of hers (or his). Will you heed my sage advice? Of course not. So let's proceed.

Picking a program

The choice of which frequent flyer program or programs to join is a function of three things: the airlines that serve your local airport, the destinations to which you fly most frequently, and the destinations to which you would like to fly on "free" frequent flyer tickets. What's more, unless you are a globetrotting businessperson, you should make every attempt to concentrate your frequent flyer miles in one airline's program — the airline offering the optimum combination of the above factors — thus giving you the greatest chance of reaping regular rewards. Many frequent travelers will find they have two programs in which they have significant mileage balances and a smattering of others in which their balances are relatively insignificant. Try to analyze your flying habits to see if you can redirect some of your travel to concentrate your mileage accrual into one or two main accounts.

If you are located in or near a hub controlled by a major airline — Delta's Atlanta, US Airway's Pittsburgh, American's Dallas, and so forth — the choice has pretty much been made for you. Otherwise, you might be able to do some shopping around. *Consumer Reports Travel Letter* rates frequent flyer programs from time to time and in 1997 found American Airlines' program to be best overall, rating it "above average" in seven of the eleven areas covered, including ease of earning benefits and destinations offered. United and Alaska Airlines tied for second, rating above average in six areas. Another tireless monitor of the frequent flyer scene is Randy Petersen, publisher of *InsideFlyer* magazine. He gives his highest grade (B+) to Northwest and American.

Every airline frequent flyer program has "partners," other airlines, hotel chains, rental car companies, and the like that give frequent flyer miles in exchange for your business. You may want to choose an airline frequent flyer program with an eye to these partners since they can help build up your mileage. Of course, the same caveats about shopping wisely apply here. If staying at the El Luxo Hotel nets you 500 frequent flyer miles, you have snagged a $5 benefit. If you stay somewhere else that charges $25 less, you have snagged a $25 benefit. Once again, expense account travelers will have fewer problems justifying a stay at the El Luxo.

There is a school of thought that holds that you should join every frequent flyer program in the world on the theory that, hey, you never know and besides a lot of them offer a mileage bonus just for signing up. If you are a truly frequent flyer, one of those globetrotting businesspeople mentioned earlier, this might make some sense. It will also help if you are extremely well organized and think creating and maintaining an elaborate file system is just a super fun thing to do with your spare time. You should also have a high tolerance for junk mail since joining a lot of programs will make you extremely attractive to direct marketers. My advice: Join a program only when you find yourself flying the airline.

Signing up for these programs is easy and you don't even have to be planning a flight to do it. Probably the best place to sign up these days in on the airline's web site, since many airlines, in an effort to train us to use the Internet, are giving special mileage bonuses for online sign-ups. But you can also call the toll-free reservation number, sign up at the airport, or even join on the plane itself in some cases.

Low-fare airlines

While this chapter is primarily about the frequent flyer programs of the major airlines, the low-fare carriers (discussed in the next chapter) have frequent flyer programs of their own, which are also worth joining. There are two major differences between the programs of the majors and the low-fare airlines:

- The major airlines award "miles," which are based on actual miles flown. The low-fare carriers award flight or segment credits. That is, for each one way trip you take, you receive one credit. Typically, the low-fare programs pay off faster than those of their high-fare competition.

- The low-fare carriers, thanks to their limited route systems, have fewer destinations to offer as awards, although that may change as low-fare carriers investigate the possibility of entering into marketing agreements with other airlines, including foreign ones, to offer more attractive award destinations.

Accumulating miles in the air

The most obvious method of accumulating miles is flying, of course, but it may not always be the best. That's because there is so often a cheaper alternative that doesn't involve frequent flyer miles and, dollar for dollar, you are always better off saving money than spending it just to add frequent flyer miles.

When your only choice is between or among major airlines, there is little to differentiate them except price, since the mileage between airports is the same no matter what airline you fly. An exception is short flights where the airline's minimum awards click in. If United and America West compete on a 400-mile flight and match each other's fares, for example, your better choice is America West, because its minimum award is 750 miles while United's is only 500. Before you drive yourself nuts trying to play these kinds of angles, however, remember that we're talking about a difference of $2.50 in the value of those miles. Hardly worth losing sleep over.

Yet if you're flying at the company's expense, you will discover sooner or later that frequent flyer miles have a way of coloring the decision-making process when it comes to choice of airline, choice of routing, choice of hotels and rental cars, and so forth. If your conscience and corporate travel policy allow you to spend the company's money with your mileage program foremost in your mind, then who am I to say you nay?

My advice to those paying their own way, on the other hand, is to fly the major airlines only when they have the best fare on a given route and let the frequent flyer miles fall where they may. An exception to this rule is the "mileage run" (see below), but that's not normal flying anyway.

Mileage runs

Airlines are constantly announcing special mileage-based promotions. Fly to London during March and get 5,000 bonus miles, for example. A bonus like this is an incentive to choose one airline over another if you happen to be traveling to London in March, but it is hardly a reason to travel just for the bonus miles.

Every once in a while, however, an airline will announce a mileage-based bonus offer with rules that make it possible to earn frequent flyer miles worth more than the amount of money you would have to pay to acquire them. This phenomenon has created a whole new category of travel with its own name — the mileage run.

A perfect example was a recent (but since expired) promotion by LatinPass, a consortium of Central and South American Airlines, that made it possible to earn a million frequent flyer miles in as little as five (very grueling) days at a cost of $2,600. Many people tried and quite a few succeeded. Of course, the saner among them spent a bit more (about $3,000) and took a little longer.

It was still worth it. Using a value of one cent per mile, a million miles is worth $10,000. A million miles could also buy 25 off-peak trips to Europe with an average value of $500, a $12,500 value in total. But consider this: A million miles could buy 12 business class tickets to Europe at an average value of $6,000. That's $72,000 worth of tickets for an expenditure of $2,600 to $3,000 and a bit of discomfort.

Of course (and unfortunately), opportunities like the LatinPass promotion don't come along very frequently, but about once a year or so a promotion pops up that makes a mileage run at least tempting.

If you want to put together your own mileage run, you'll need to keep your ear to the frequent flyer grapevine (see the Further Reading chapter) and have a taste for poring over fine print. You must also plan your itinerary with care. Booking in the wrong fare code can negate your eligibility, as can flying the wrong airline partner between specific cities.

For most normal people it will make sense to work with a

knowledgeable travel agent. One agent who specializes in mileage runs is Brian Maule of Tango Travel Consulting in Poulsbo, WA. He charges a premium for his services but you will still make out like a bandit and have the added assurance of knowing that all the arrangements have been made just so. Brian provides his clients on mileage runs with detailed instructions and sometimes leads groups himself.

If you'd like to be notified by email when Brian spots a good mileage run opportunity, send him an email message at twotango@home.com.

Accumulating miles on the ground

If mileage runs are not your cup of tea and if you don't fly every week on business, you might think that you'll have to wait years between "free" trips on your mileage awards. Think again. There are plenty of ways to accumulate frequent flyer miles without flying and a lot of them make perfect economic sense.

Airline credit cards

Every major airline now has a branded "affinity" credit card that lets you accumulate mileage as you spend money on things you'd be buying anyway. All of them give one frequent flyer mile for every dollar spent. So if you spend $100 a week on groceries and pay for them with your airline affinity card, you'll get 5,200 frequent flyer miles for money you'd spend anyway. If you have a small business, the miles can add up rapidly when you charge major capital expenditures and regular monthly expenses. My advice would be to investigate all the ways in which you can shift cash and check payments to your airline affinity card. If you spend a lot of money each year, you can easily get one or two "free" trips. But beware! This is not an invitation to go into debt. All of these cards charge very high interest (although many of them offer a six-month interest-free introductory period) and no frequent flyer miles are given on finance charges or cash advances. If you pay off your entire balance every month, terrific. If not, think twice about whether this strategy makes sense for you. Here are some additional considerations:

- *Silver or Gold.* Most cards come in two flavors, plain vanilla and Gold. The "gold" card has a higher annual fee but may allow you to accumulate more mileage (see below). Surprisingly, only a few gold cards offer a lower percentage rate in exchange for the higher fee. Gold cards will also have additional bells and whistles like higher insurance coverage and the like; read the fine print carefully to make sure the additional cost is worth it to you. In general, the gold card will only make sense if you know you are going to be charging more than $60,000 a year to the card.

- *Mileage caps.* The plain-vanilla cards usually have an annual cap in the 60,000 range on the number of frequent flyer miles you can accumulate; the Gold cards sometimes, but not always, offer a higher cap. And some are cap-free.

- *Annual fees.* All cards have annual fees, although some may waive the first year's fee. Fees for regular cards range from about $30 to $60; fees for Gold cards range from about $45 to $100. The annual fee determines the actual "cost" of the frequent flyer miles you accumulate each year. For most acquisitive Americans, the per mile cost will be well under a penny. For example, if the annual fee is $50 and you charge just $6,000 a year (6,000 miles), the per mile cost is about eight tenths of a cent.

- *Enrollment bonuses.* Most cards give you a mileage bonus of anywhere from 1,000 to 5,000. One Gold card even gives 10,000 miles.

By now you should know which of the airline mileage programs will work best for you. Here are the credit cards linked to them. Most will let you apply over the phone, but I would encourage you to ask them to send complete information so you can pore over the always entertaining fine print.

Alaska Airlines (MasterCard and Visa); (800) 442-6680
America West (Visa); (800) 508-2933
American Airlines (MasterCard and Visa); (800) 359-4444
Continental Airlines (MasterCard and Visa); (800) 377-0601

Delta Airlines (American Express); (800) 759-6453
Midwest Express (MasterCard); (800) 388-4044
Northwest Airlines (Visa); (800) 360-2900
Southwest Airlines (Visa); (800) 792-8472
TWA (MasterCard and Visa); (800) 523-7666
United Airlines (MasterCard and Visa); (800) 537-7783
US Airways (Visa); (800) 294-0849

Other travel credit cards

In addition to airline affinity cards, there are a number of credit card products that offer benefits to air travelers, although not always in the form of mileage. Making a decision on these cards is nowhere near as straightforward as with the airline affinity cards, so investigate carefully before deciding if one or more of these cards might work for you.

Amex Membership Rewards
(800) 297-3276
Earn miles that can be transferred to various airline frequent flyer programs for redemption. It costs $75 a year for a corporate account and $40 a year for an individual.

Amex Platinum
(800) 525-3355
It costs a whopping $300 a year but gives you membership in Continental's and Northwest's hoity-toity airport lounges, which more than pays for the card membership. There are many other benefits, including two for one offers for business and first class international travel on 14 airlines. Probably worth it for the high-rolling frequent traveler.

Amex Student Privileges
(800) 582-5823
Gives college and graduate students some Continental discount coupons and 30 minutes of free MCI long distance each month.

Chase Flight Rewards
(800) 581-7770
25,000 points gets you a $500 domestic ticket on the

airline of your choice; if the ticket's more expensive, you can pay the difference.

Diners Club Club Rewards

(800) 234-6377

Another pooled mileage card for 20 airlines.

Elton John AIDS Foundation Visa

(800) 523-5866

Earn credit towards free travel while a portion of each purchase goes towards battling AIDS.

First USA Platinum

(800) 955-9900

The usual one mile for one dollar, except when you book travel through them. In that case you get three miles per dollar. Redeem 24,000 miles for a domestic trip.

FirstAir Classic Card (Visa)

(800) 835-9373

Your choice of airlines for awards, plus a 5,000-mile sign-up bonus.

Hawaii Advantage Visa

(800) 342-2778

Build credit toward travel to Hawaii.

MasterCard Cardmiles

(800) 927-0100

For every 5,000 points, receive a $25 rebate on any airline ticket. For every 25,000 points, receive a free airline ticket.

MBNA Platinum

(800) 739-5554

This one gives you a 50% mileage credit for balances carried over from month to month. Requires 35,000 miles for a domestic trip.

Travel Choices Visa

(800) 349-2632

Gives you a choice of several airlines for award travel. 25,000 miles for a domestic trip, 40,000 to the Caribbean or Mexico, 50,000 to Europe.

TravelMax Visa

(800) 858-0905

If you pay your full balance each month, you get one mile for each $3 spent; carry a balance and get one for one. Travel awards are based on zones. You call them and tell them where you want to go; they'll book you on the airline offering them the cheapest fare.

Wells Fargo BusinessCard (MasterCard)
(800) 359-3557

This program lets small business owners give credit cards to all their employees and reap the mileage rewards up to a maximum of 180,000 miles per business per year. Mileage is redeemed through an in-house travel department and there is some choice of airline.

Eating miles

You gotta eat, right? So why not rack up miles while you chew? The key variables to look for in airline dining programs are the number of participating restaurants and the number of miles awarded per dollar spent (tip and taxes not included). In both cases, the more the better. There are two variations in these programs. In one, you register a specific credit card with the program. Each time you use that card at a participating restaurant, your miles get automatically credited to your account. In the other variation, you give the waiter a card from the program itself. This card is in turn linked to a specific credit card number of yours and your bill will appear on that card's statement. Note that the credit card you use can be an airline affinity card, thus adding another mile per dollar to your haul.

AAdvantage Dining
(800) 804-4372

American Airline's program has 6,500 participating restaurants and pays ten miles per dollar, with no annual fee. You can register up to three credit cards with this program.

Dining a la Card
(800) 555-5396
www.dalc.com

This company operates the dining programs of a number of airlines (including the ones listed separately here) and offers the convenience of one-stop shopping. You can call up and register your frequent flyer number for the dining programs of America West, American, British Airways, Continental, Northwest, TWA, US Airways, or United. You must register a different credit card (or cards) for each. Membership is complimentary and you receive 10 frequent flyer miles per dollar spent at participating restaurants.

SkyMiles Dining
(800) 498-0548
Earn three miles per dollar at participating restaurants when you show your SkyMiles membership card.

United Mileage Plus Dining
(800) 555-5116
This program has 6,500 participating restaurants and pays 10 miles per dollar, with no annual fee. Register up to three cards.

WorldPerks Dining for Miles
(800) 818-2040
This Northwest program has over 5,000 participating restaurants and pays 10 miles per dollar including tax and tip, with no annual fee. Only the first visit each month to a restaurant qualifies for miles but you can earn up to 6,000 miles on that visit. Register up to three credit cards.

Miles for investors

Now you can even earn miles when you play the stock market, safely of course, through mutual funds. Warburg Pincus Asset Management offers one Northwest WorldPerks mile for every $4 invested on an annual basis in two of its money market funds. Contact Warburg at (800) 927-2874 or on the Internet at www.warburg.com.

American Airlines has set up AAdvantage Mileage Funds, seven no-load mutual funds that earn miles. They include growth and income, international equity, and bond funds in addition to money market funds. Contact them at (800) 388-3344 or www.aafunds.com.

Miles on the house

Six airlines participate in programs that let you earn miles when you buy or sell a house. Some even pay miles on mortgages. The catch, of course, is that you have to funnel your business through certain brokers or mortgage lenders. That's fine if you feel you are getting the best deal possible, but with the large numbers involved in home purchases (and especially in mortgage interest) these deals require careful scrutiny and the input of your legal and financial advisors. Note that some programs are not available in all states.

American Airlines
(800) 852-9744

This program pays miles on mortgage interest through participating lenders. It also provides 15,000 miles per $100,000 on the purchase or sale of a house through a participating broker.

Continental Airlines
(800) 732-7391

Earn from 12,500 to 125,000 miles on the purchase or sale of a home.

Delta Airlines
(800) 759-0306

Get 1,000 miles for every $10,000 you borrow. There is no limit on the number of miles you can earn (presumably a $10 million mortgage would net a million miles) and it also works when refinancing.

Northwest Airlines
(888) 644-6639

Earn from 12,500 to 125,000 miles on the purchase or sale of a home. Get 1,000 miles per $10,000 borrowed, or 1,750 per $10,000 on a home equity loan.

TWA
(800) 654-5409

Earn from 10,000 to 40,000 miles on the purchase or sale of a home.

United Airlines
(800) 717-5330

Earn from 3,000 to 120,000 miles on the purchase or sale of a home. Get 1,000 miles per $10,000 on a refinancing. Mileage deals vary on first mortgages.

Dialing for miles

MCI and Sprint both offer deals that pay five frequent flyer miles for every dollar spent on their residential services. Businesses are not eligible. AT&T had discontinued a similar program at press time.

In my opinion, these programs are less attractive than the ones listed above because you can get better long distance rates elsewhere and apply the savings toward future travel. For example, if you are paying ten cents a minute with MCI or Sprint and have a $250 monthly long distance bill, you earn 1,250 miles a month. But if you were paying 7.5 cents a minute, your monthly bill would be just $187.50. You are, in effect, paying $62.50 for those frequent flyer miles or five cents each, which as we have seen is no great bargain. Of course, there is always the possibility that MCI and Sprint will lower their per-minute charges, making these plans more attractive.

If you're still interested, contact MCI at (800) 200-9007 or Sprint at (800) 746-3767.

Accumulating miles in cyberspace

There are a growing number of ways to collect frequent flyer miles — or their rough equivalent — by logging on to the Internet. Here are some of the more prominent ones:

Milesource

Now you can collect miles in cyberspace. Milesource.com offers a program that makes it easy for online merchants to offer frequent flyer miles as an incentive to shop on the Internet. Some big players like Amazon and OfficeMax already participate and more can be expected to follow.

Once you have joined Milesource (it's free), you enter participating merchants through the Milesource site and go shopping. The standard deal is one AwardMile, as they are called, for each dollar spent at a participating online merchant (shipping not included). At press time, Milesource was offering a "limited time only" deal of two AwardMiles per dollar spent. In addition, Milesource has a feature called the Click Arcade. There you can earn one AwardMile simply for clicking through to any of the twenty-some sites listed, and you can collect an AwardMile for visiting a site once each day. There are other ways to earn AwardMiles that seem to come and go.

The real lure of Milesource, however, lies in its referral program. You receive ten percent of the AwardMiles earned by anyone you sign up and 5% of the AwardMiles anyone they sign up earns, and so on through four levels. If you have the means to reach a lot of people (a web site, for example), the potential exists to start receiving a substantial number of "passive income" AwardMiles. I have tried it and so far it seems to be working.

There are few downsides. A minimum of 25,000 AwardMiles is required for a domestic ticket and AwardMiles aren't transferable to your existing frequent flyer accounts. You can redeem your AwardMiles only through Milesource for tickets on one of their participating airlines. You can, however, redeem lesser amounts of AwardMiles for gift certificates.

Freeairmiles.com

A miles-for-clicks model is offered by Freeairmiles.com (www.freeairmiles.com). At the site, registered users are rewarded with one to five "miles" for clicking on links to advertisers, much like Milesource's ClickArcade, except that here you can earn up to 100 miles in any 24-hour period.

The miles accumulated are not, strictly speaking, frequent flyer miles. Instead, they can be redeemed only through Freeairmiles.com's partnership with 1Travel.com, an online travel agency. A specified number of miles is needed to "purchase" a ticket (or other travel product, presumably) within a specified dollar range. Miles can also be redeemed for gift certificates at online merchants such as Amazon.com.

Freeairmiles.com also has a referral program, but you are rewarded just five miles for signing up a new web surfer and you do not get a share of the miles they generate.

ClickRewards

ClickRewards is older than Milesource and, in my opinion, a less attractive alternative, although the concept is similar — miles for shopping.

The first step is to join ClickRewards either at their site (www.clickrewards.com) or via one of their participating merchants. Each time you shop or rather each time you make a "qualifying purchase" at a participating site you earn ClickMiles, which are automatically added to your ClickRewards account and accumulate with no expiration date. ClickRewards keeps track of your mileage on their site and you can review your account by entering your password. When you are ready to cash in your miles you can go to the ClickRewards site and transfer some or all of your accumulated miles (500-mile minimum) to any of seven airline frequent flyer programs. You must be a member of the airline frequent flyer program before you can transfer ClickMiles into it. One ClickMile equals one frequent flyer mile.

One complicating factor is that each merchant seems to handle ClickMiles a bit differently. I have yet to see a one-to-one relationship (i.e. one ClickMile for each dollar spent). Rather you seem to get bunches of ClickMiles for reaching a certain dollar level in your purchases. Recently, at Barnes and Noble, for example, you got 50 ClickMiles for spending $50 and 150 for spending $250. But if you spent $57 or $249, you still got only 50; if you spent $49, you got nothing. On the other hand, you could buy a $15 book from WebFlyer (www.webflyer.com) and get 250 ClickMiles. Obviously, you will need to check each offer to see what makes sense. Use the "one mile is worth one cent" formula when making your decision.

More mileage ploys

There are many other ways to add to your stash of frequent flyer miles and some of them won't cost you a penny. Frequent flyer miles have become a popular premium to entice folks to buy or take some other action. Airlines are giving miles for on-line bookings to encourage people to bypass their travel agents. You can collect frequent flyer miles for filling out a survey on the

Internet. You can even get miles when you buy a car from a dealer.

Offers like these come and go, so finding out about them can be a haphazard affair. Readers of *Best Fares* and *InsideFlyer* magazines (see Chapter Ten) will get the latest information on a monthly basis or through their web sites (www.bestfares.com and www.insideflyer.com). Since many frequent flyer opportunities are cropping up on the Internet, a cottage industry of fan sites has sprung up to track down mile-earning opportunities and spread the word. You may even get some pointers on sneaky ways to pick up extra miles from the airlines. It's simple enough to find these sites. Just go to a few of the major search engines and type in "frequent flyer mile." You'll find plenty of sites, but what you are looking for are the sites set up by frequent flyer fanatics. Here are a few I've come across. Just bear in mind that since these are maintained by individuals, they may have moved or disappeared by the time you try to find them.

www.toolcity.net/~sgiesler/index.html
members.tripod.com/~SportAid/index.html
www.mileageworkshop.com

Minding your miles

As long as you are going to the trouble of building your frequent flyer mileage account, you might as well go the whole distance and take the trouble to make sure you're getting what's coming to you. If you are naturally well organized this shouldn't be too much of a problem. If you're like me, you'll probably just take it on faith that the monthly accountings you receive are accurate and let it go at that. Most of the time they are.

However, you should take some basic precautions. First of all, have a file folder for each frequent flyer program in which you are enrolled and file your statements each month. It's a good idea to keep them for at least several months, but at some point you will want to begin discarding the oldest when you file the latest. It's also a good idea to hang on to your boarding pass stubs and drop them in the file. That way, if a trip you took doesn't get posted to your account, you will have backup. Never send original boarding passes when corresponding with the program, send photocopies.

Tracking mileage from your affinity credit cards is pretty straightforward. It's a matter of comparing last month's credit card bill with this month's posted mileage. If there's a discrepancy, remember that finance charges and cash advances don't receive mileage credit. Tracking the other odds and ends is more problematic, especially things like the 500 miles you're supposed to get for filling out that survey on the Internet. You might want to make notes in your appointment book or diary as you travel and then later transfer those notes to the appropriate file folder to compare against your next statement. Or you may just want to forget it.

One thing you shouldn't forget is that, with some exceptions, you cannot keep racking up miles indefinitely. Today many mileage awards are good for just three years, at which point they disappear. Most programs are pretty good about calling out on their monthly reports the expiration dates of various groups of miles you have earned. If you have a bunch of miles expiring at the end of the year, you may be able to get an extension by calling the program. You can also get either a confirmed ticket or a certificate on the very last day before those miles expire and have up to a year to use it. Miles are cashed in beginning with the oldest. So if you have 8,000 miles expiring this year and choose a 25,000-mile award, the first 8,000 miles will be deducted from the soon-to-expire mileage, thus wiping out that portion of your account. The remaining 17,000 miles will be deducted from the next most elderly batch of miles.

If you are a very frequent flyer with membership in many programs, it may be worth your while to enroll in the Internet-based MaxMiles MileageMiner program. Give them your frequent flyer numbers and they will stay on top of them for you, posting regular reports to a secure site on the web where you (and only you) can check them at your leisure. They provide a summary of your mileage, an "expiration analysis," and detailed information on where every last mile came from. You can sign up at www.maxmiles.com. There is a three-month free trial period, after which they will charge you $29.95 per year.

After your final flight

Frequent flyer miles are an asset and like any other asset they can be passed on to your heirs in the case of your death. To do this cleanly and legally, you need to list the beneficiary in your will. It will also be helpful to include a list of your frequent flyer program membership numbers.

Spending your miles

The dirty little secret of frequent flyer miles is that there are so few seats available for all those "free" trips you're entitled to. The airlines have steadfastly resisted revealing the actual number of seats they set aside to fulfill frequent flyer awards, but it is probably no more than a few on each flight. Compare that to the billions of frequent flyer miles waiting to be redeemed and you begin to understand the rising chorus of complaints from customers who say they can never seem to get the trips they're entitled to. Actually, it could be worse. According to Tom Parsons of *Best Fares* Magazine, only 15% of all frequent flyer miles accumulated are ever redeemed. If this is accurate, you have to ask yourself again why people constantly choose frequent flyer miles over price when making their travel arrangements.

The moral of the story is plan ahead. The further in advance you arrange your travel, the better the odds of finding a seat. I regularly book my award travel six or more months in advance and — knock wood — have always gotten my first choice of dates. Here are some other tips for spending your miles wisely:

- *Do it now.* Not only do some frequent flyer miles expire, but the amount required for any given award can change without notice. Remember that you can lock in a trip almost a full year before you actually take it. (Usually, the trip must be completed within one year of booking.)
- *Jump on sales.* Airlines have sales on frequent flyer awards just as they do on regular fares. Read the little brochures that come with your monthly statements and move quickly when you spot something good.

- **Choose long trips.** There's little point in using a frequent flyer award for a short trip that you could take on a low-cost airline. Fly cross-country or overseas instead.
- **Be flexible.** Work with the airline to find which dates or flights will let you use your award mileage.
- **Use open jaws when possible.** Flying into Helsinki and back from Istanbul will often cost no more miles than a roundtrip to either city, and you gain a great deal of flexibility.
- **Remember the partners.** If your airline can't accommodate you, maybe one of its frequent flyer partners has availability on an appealing route.
- **Fly off-season.** One reason people report difficulty in finding seats for their award travel is that most people want to travel at the same time. If you can be a contrarian, you will have better luck finding space. Spring and Fall are good times to try since they offer a combination of reduced demand and good weather. Of course, the tradeoff is that in the off-season, your frequent flyer miles are worth less since fares are lower.
- **Buy upgrades.** Using your frequent flyer miles to fly in business or first class on a paid-for coach ticket can be very cost-effective. Do a cost analysis to see.
- **Fly business class.** If you have so many miles that you are unlikely to use them all for coach travel, why not be nice to yourself? On many airlines, 240,000 miles equals either four coach or three business tickets to Europe.
- **Try for last-minute deals.** Before forking over big bucks for a short-notice trip, check to see if you can use your frequent flyer miles. If the flight is not selling well, the airline just may have released some seats for award travel.
- **Use cost analysis in making your decisions.** I mentioned earlier that frequent flyer miles tend to be worth about a penny, but if you spend them wisely they can be worth as much as two cents or even more.

When planning a trip on frequent flyer miles, determine the best price available on the open market at the time of booking. Then divide the number of award miles needed to take the trip for "free" to find the per mile value of your miles.

A final thought

If you are one of those people who keeps racking up frequent flyer miles and never seems to get around to using them, consider donating them to charity. You should make a special point of doing this with miles that are going to expire before you have any hope of using them. Many programs let you give miles to heartwarming causes like providing air travel to ailing children. Call your airline's frequent flyer department to ask about procedures. Better to light a single candle than curse the loss of your miles.

Chapter Four

Low-Fare Airlines

In 1978, the United States Congress passed the Airline Deregulation Act, which allowed airlines to set their own fares and compete more readily for routes. It also became much easier to start new airlines. How successful deregulation has been depends, to some extent, on which end of the political spectrum you sit. Conservatives point out that the average cost of an airline ticket has decreased 9% in the 20 years or so since deregulation. Liberals like to point out that deregulation has concentrated equity ownership while sending CEO salaries and stock options skyrocketing.

One fact is beyond dispute: deregulation gave birth to a whole new category of airline, the low-fare carrier. These upstarts competed aggressively against the major airlines by offering no-frills service at low, low fares. The major airlines responded in free market fashion and lowered their own fares usually to precisely match those of the new low-price competition. What a great deal for everyone.

Except that the low-fare airlines kept going out of business. People's Express, Markair, Western Pacific, Kiwi, and others once offered super fares on the routes they served, but they are no more. Obviously a great many factors contribute to any business failure, but one common thread in all these failures was the major airlines' attempts to run the little guys out of business and the alacrity with which they raised fares when they succeeded.

Did I say that? Perish the thought. The men who run these airlines are honorable fellows all and would be horrified at any suggestion that they engage in predatory competitive practices. Nonetheless, suspicions persist. For example, when Western Pacific went belly up, the cost of a ticket between Denver and Seattle shot up 600% overnight.

The point, gentle reader, is that the low-fare airlines are the budget traveler's friend and they deserve your support and patronage. The major airlines will invariably match a low-fare carrier's fares on routes where they compete. They may also have more, and more convenient, departures. They will almost certainly have more advertising dollars at their disposal to inform you about their fares and their schedules. Their planes may be a little bigger, their seating modestly more comfortable. Their meal service might provide stale sandwiches instead of mere peanuts. Their frequent flyer program may be able to get you to Paris while the low-fare carrier's frequent flyer program will only get you to Podunk again. They may even offer bonus frequent flyer miles on their competing flights to woo you to their planes. And you might just allow yourself be wooed.

I don't want to make you a villain if you succumb, but be aware of the potential consequences, because when the low-priced alternative goes under due to your lack of patronage, the major airline will reward you with sharply higher fares.

Thus endeth the sermon.

What's a low-fare airline?

Low-fare airlines are not charitable institutions. In order to charge low fares, they have to hold down costs. Some of these cost cutting strategies are the sorts of thing the traveler will never notice; others are fairly obvious, even to the most casual observer. Here, then, are some of the things that set low-fare airlines apart from the big guys.

- *Limited routes.* Many low-fare airlines stick very close to the hub-and-spoke model. That is, most of their flights radiate out from a central airport; reaching most if not all of their destinations means traveling through the hub, often changing planes in the process.
- *Limited seating options.* Many low-fare carriers use an

all-coach seating configuration, and a cramped one at that. Some, however, advertise their roomier seats.

- *Limited service.* Low-fare carriers typically offer fewer daily departures than the big guys. On top of that, once aloft, meal service may be nonexistent and there may be fewer flight attendants to call on. Some low-fare carriers have turned their lean staffing to their advantage by encouraging a breezy informality among their flight attendants and pilots, which can make flying these airlines a lot of fun.
- *Simplified fare structures.* In place of the Byzantine fares of the majors, low-fare carriers have substituted a pared down system. Typically there are three fares on each route pegged to how far in advance you purchase your ticket. A 14-day advance purchase gets the lowest fare, 7 days the middle fare, and anything up to flight time the highest.
- *Capacity-controlled pricing.* Some low-fare airlines have a tiered fare system, with a certain number of seats per flight pegged to each fare. The first seats sold on any given flight are sold at the lowest fare. When a predetermined number of seats are sold, the fare jumps to the next tier. The final block of seats sold is sold at the highest fare. Invariably, the price advertised on a given route will be the lowest price, but the price you actually get for a specific flight on a specific date might be higher.
- *Ticketless travel.* One way to hold down costs is to dispense with printed tickets. Not all low-fare carriers do this, but many do.
- *No assigned seats.* The same is true of assigned seating. Some low-fare carriers assign numbers to arriving passengers on a first-come, first-served basis and then board passengers in numerical order, letting them pick their own seats.
- *Limited frequent flyer programs.* Low-fare airlines have frequent flyer programs, they are just not as fancy as the ones sponsored by the major airlines. Typically

they are based on segments flown, rather than distance. It takes anywhere from 12 to 18 segments to earn a free roundtrip anywhere in the carrier's system. Some low-fare carriers are trying to offer award travel outside their own route system to make their programs more attractive.

- *Older, smaller planes.* Used planes are cheaper, just like used cars. Unlike many used cars, however, the planes flown by these carriers are meticulously maintained and in perfect flying condition. In spite of some hysterical media coverage that suggests otherwise, there is no hard evidence that low-fare airlines are any less safe than major airlines. Most of the low-fare carriers now boast an all-jet fleet, although on some shorter "commuter" flights you can still expect to fly on a turboprop aircraft. If this is the sort of thing that bothers you, ask about the equipment being flown when you call about reservations.

Using low-fare airlines

Use it or lose it. I am a big booster of the low-fare airlines and I urge you to become one too. If you followed my earlier advice, you have made a survey of the airlines serving your local airport and have collected their schedules and route maps. If your area is served by a low-fare carrier, congratulations. Study the destinations available to you and take advantage of their service whenever possible.

While I urge you to fly the low-fare carriers all the time as a matter of principle, there are circumstances in which choosing the low-fare alternative are especially attractive:

- *Short business trips.* Major airlines may match the fares of the low-fare carriers, but often only for leisure travelers, that is folks who will be staying through Saturday night at their destination. If you are faced with making a two- or three-day business trip, the low-fare airline's fare structure will almost always be the obvious winner.

- ***Short notice trips.*** Similar savings will be found when you have to fly on relatively short notice and you've missed the 7-, 14-, or 21-day advance purchase requirements the major airlines place on leisure fares.
- ***One way flights.*** You are probably already savvy to the ploy the major airlines use when advertising their fares: at the bottom of the ad, in teeny print, is the disclaimer "one way, based on roundtrip purchase." If you actually want to fly one way, the one way fare skyrockets. There is a school of thought that holds that this is deceptive advertising, like advertising a car for $5,000 and then explaining in a footnote that this is a per-seat cost price based on the purchase of a five-seat car. But airlines seem to escape the straightforward logic that applies to other merchants.

What if the low-fare carrier serving your area, doesn't fly where you want to go? If you're a dedicated budget traveler and are willing to trade some time and convenience, you may be able to stitch together a journey on two low-fare carriers. For example, I just checked availability on a midweek trip (i.e. no Saturday night stay) and found that I could fly from New York's LaGuardia airport to Kansas City, via Chicago/Midway, using ATA and Vanguard Airlines. The total roundtrip cost: $380. The alternative would be to fly on Midwest Express or US Airways for about $805 roundtrip.

Two low-fare airlines won't inevitably be cheaper than one major airline. In the LaGuardia-Kansas City example just cited, I could have opted to fly from Newark on Delta, with a change of plane in Atlanta, and made the midweek journey for $352. Of course, the taxi fare to Newark would have more than erased the savings. Like the song says, you gotta shop around.

Another way to use low-fare airlines is to hopscotch around the country using a series of one way tickets on any number of low-fare airlines. I suspect that salespeople and others in business use this ploy when plotting a series of calls on customers or prospects, but I wonder how many people think of this when planning their vacations. It's conceivable that someone in Chicago could spend the first half of a two-week vacation swimming in

113

sunny Florida, then pop over for some skiing in the Rockies, with a stop for barbecue in Kansas City en route, and then return to the Windy City. And use four different low-fare airlines to do it! For foreign visitors especially, low-fare airlines offer an unparalleled opportunity to explore the country at bargain rates.

Domestic low-fare airlines

On the following pages, I list the low-fare carriers operating in the United States at press time, along with brief comments on each. For those of you who are interested, I have provided the two-letter codes for each airline, when available. The code lets you locate the airline quickly in a computerized reservation system (CRS) — assuming of course the airline's flights are listed in the CRS. Not all of the low-fare airlines are willing to pay the price to be listed in these systems, which are owned, perhaps not incidentally, by the major airlines.

Be aware, also, that the destinations offered by low-fare airlines change frequently. Of course, by the time you read this, the list of airlines may have changed. It may have grown. Or the big, bad major airlines may have driven some of the carriers listed here into the wild blue yonder of ex-airlines. Let's hope not.

AirTran (FL)

800-247-8726
www.airtran.com

AirTran connects the Northeast and the upper Midwest to the Gulf Coast and Florida through its hub in Atlanta. It also flies between Boston, Washington, and Chicago. AirTran advertises the "fastest free ticket on earth" through its frequent flyer program. It also offers standby fares to those 18 to 22.

American Trans Air (TZ)

(800) 225-2995
www.ata.com

American Trans Air has been around for a quarter of a century, linking its Chicago and Indianapolis hubs with warm-weather destinations like Hawaii, Florida, and Puerto Rico. It is one of the few low-fare airlines with a foreign destination, Cancun, Mexico. It offers a 10% senior discount, ticketless online booking, commuter books, and weekly web specials. Chicago Express, a subsidiary, operates some feeder flights into Chicago.

Delta Express (DL)

(800) 325-5205
www.delta-air.com/express/

Delta has met the low-fare challenge by creating its own, separate low-fare carrier, and it seems to be making a success of it. Using Orlando, FL, as its hub, Delta Express covers the Northeast and Midwest from there and four other Florida cities. All flights from Orlando are nonstop and single-class, with a three-tiered fare structure (21-day, 7-day, and walk-up).

Frontier (F9)

(800) 432-1359
www.flyfrontier.com

Here's a low-fare airline that can get you all the way across the country, with a stop and perhaps a change of plane in Denver. It also has a frequent flyer program that partners with Continental, giving you a wide choice of award travel. There is no online booking, but special sales are occasionally announced on its web site and it does give seniors (62+) and a companion of any age an across-the-board 10% discount. Frontier has a special program aimed at business travelers.

JetBlue (B6)

(800) 538-2583
www.jetblue.com

JetBlue is an unusually well-capitalized start-up based at New York's JFK airport. It currently flies to Buffalo, Rochester, Tampa, Orlando, and Ft. Lauderdale, as well as Los Angeles and San Francisco. Eventually, it hopes to service 30 cities.

JetBlue is ticketless and its slick web site offers online booking. Fares have three levels: 14-day advance, 7-day advance, and walk-up. Sample fares from New York to Tampa were recently $79, $119, and $159, respectively. At press time, the lowest transcontinental fare was $99. All fares are one way and no roundtrip purchase is required. JetBlue flies Airbus 320s in a one-class configuration with "roomy leather seats." Seat-back satellite television is available for $5.

Legend Airlines (LC)

(877) 359-5343

www.legendairlines.com

Legend Airlines is a low-fare airline only in the sense that its ultra-luxury level of service would cost a lot more from one of the major airlines. Even then, it's unlikely any of the airlines flying out of Dallas-Ft. Worth (DFW) airport matches Legend's posh configuration.

Legend flies out of Dallas' close-in Love Field and its 56-seat configuration is designed to finesse a law created specifically to give DFW a monopoly in flights to cities outside Texas. Legend offers one-class, two-abreast leather seating with plenty of legroom and a carry-on policy that allows four bags per passenger. There's also upscale airline food served on real china. All of this luxury is reasonably affordable considering that Legend attempts to match coach fares out of DFW to the three destinations it currently serves: Washington-Dulles, Los Angeles, and Las Vegas. Legend has its own frequent flyer program (25,000 miles for a free roundtrip) and miles can also be redeemed on Delta.

Metrojet (US)

(888) 638-7653

www.flymetrojet.com

Metrojet is US Airways version of Delta Express, that is, a low-fare airline within a high-fare airline. Its route system provides pretty comprehensive coverage east of the Mississippi, although it conspicuously bypasses New York. It is ticketless and single class but assigns seats at the gate on its Boeing 737-200s. Fares are either 14-day advance purchase or walk-up.

Metrojet's frequent flyer program is integrated with US Airways. You can either earn double miles on US Airways or accumulate segment credits plus regular miles. In the second option, you can earn a Metrojet roundtrip for 16 segment credits and simultaneously have the Metrojet mileage applied toward a US Airways award.

Midway (JI)

(800) 446-4392
www.midwayair.com

Operating from its hub in Raleigh/Durham, NC, Midway serves the eastern seaboard from Boston to Florida, with one stop each in Ohio (Columbus) and Indiana (Indianapolis). It is one of the more financially successful of the low-fare carriers and has an eclectic fleet of regional jets. A first class cabin is offered on the larger planes. Its frequent flyer program has a tie in with American Airlines, allowing you to redeem award travel on either airline. Midway prides itself on its level of service, which includes such niceties as all-leather seats and hot towels on all flights.

National Airlines (N7)

(888) 757-5387
www.nationalairlines.com

This Las Vegas-based carrier offers service to San Francisco, Los Angeles, Chicago, Newark, New York (JFK), Philadelphia, Dallas, and Miami, and promises low fares and "spacious seating." Transcontinental flights often offer free Vegas stopovers. It is partially owned by some Vegas hoteliers, so look for attractive packages with luggage delivered to your hotel. It uses electronic ticketing and provides online booking at its web site. Its Boeing 757s are configured for two classes. The deepest savings (percentage-wise) will be found on first class and unrestricted coach fares, something that should appeal to the business traveler.

Pro Air (P9)

(800) 477-6247
www.proair.com

Detroit-based Pro Air made some airline history by entering into a flat-fee agreement with General Motors and Chrysler that gives employees of the two automotive giants something akin to a free pass on selected Pro Air flights, a neat solution to the high cost of business travel. From Detroit it serves a limited list of business destinations like Chicago, New York, Baltimore, and Atlanta, but there are also flights to Orlando. Pro Air is ticketless, charges one flat fare per segment regardless of when tickets are purchased, and uses a fleet of Boeing 737s configured for two classes of service. Recently, Pro Air was offering a one way, web-only Detroit-New York fare of $59.

Shuttle America (S5)

(888) 999-3273
www.shuttleamerica.com

One of the smallest of the low-fares, Shuttle America offers point-to-point service between Buffalo, NY, Hartford, CT, Boston, MA, Trenton, NJ, and Greensboro, NC, using 50-seat Dash 8-300 turboprops with all leather interiors. Fares are three-tiered (14-day, 7-day, and walk-up), but some routes offer "weekender fares" that may occasionally be available midweek as well.

Shuttle America also offers a "Name Your Price" option. If you round up a group of more than three people, you may be able to get a fare lower than the lowest published fare.

Southwest Airlines (WN)

(800) 435-9792
www.iflyswa.com

Southwest is the granddaddy of all low-fare airlines and one of the most successful and popular airlines in the country. With its coast-to-coast reach and long list of destinations it is, in fact, a major airline — except for the fares.

Southwest is completely ticketless and decidedly no-frills — passengers are handed numbers when they arrive at the gate to determine the order of boarding — yet the airline has received consistently high ratings from the flying public. The airline also has a frequent flyer program, a branded credit card, and an in-house tour operator.

Spirit (NK)

(800) 772-7117
www.spiritair.com

Spirit links northern cities like Detroit, New York and Atlantic City with Myrtle Beach, NC, and several Florida cities; there is also point-to-point service between Detroit and Los Angeles and Cleveland and Atlantic City. Fares on the one-class carrier are capacity controlled and it has only recently been assigning seats. Spirit offers three-day casino packages to Atlantic City from Cleveland, Myrtle Beach, and West Palm Beach, starting at $199. Bookings can be made online and the airline offers "Syber Specials" featuring one way fares as low as $59.

Sun Country (SY)

(800) 752-1218

www.suncountry.com

From its Minneapolis hub, Sun Country flies mostly to the south, including as far south as Aruba and Costa Rica, making it one of the few low-fare carriers with foreign destinations. There are also some northern business destinations offered, such as Detroit, Milwaukee, Boston, New York, and Washington, as well as San Francisco, Los Angeles, and several Florida cities. It is a one-class airline and there are about six fares per flight depending on both availability and how far in advance you book.

Sun Country's "onefare" program offers businesses a set per-segment fare of $130 to any domestic destination in return for a commitment to make at least 40 segments in a year; the tickets can be used by any employee or family member, even by the company's vendors. The program would probably work best for companies based in Minneapolis and restrictions, as they say, apply. Sun Country also offers "Cy-Fly Fares" and online booking. A companion web site, www.heybill.com, offers occasional wacky promotions.

Vanguard (NJ)

(800) 826-4827

www.flyvanguard.com

Vanguard is ticketless and operates a fleet of Boeing 737s from its hub in Kansas City. It offers 14-day, 7-day, 1-day, and walk-up fares to Denver, Dallas, Atlanta, Minneapolis, Chicago (MDW), and Pittsburgh. It also serves Myrtle Beach, NC and New Orleans. Fares start at $89 one way and sales can drop fares on shorter runs to $29. It has both a "Road Warrior" program offering flexibility and other perks to business travelers and a frequent flyer program that awards one free roundtrip for 16 one way segments flown within a 12-month period.

WestJet (WS)

(888) 937-8538
www.westjet.com

This Canadian low-fare carrier is based in Calgary and offers service to 14 major cities, mostly in Canada's west although it also serves Ottawa, Hamilton, and Moncton in the east. Online booking is available and WestJet's "Special Fares" can drop one way fares as low as $50 (Canadian).

Some low-fare wannabes

The low-fare carrier category is remarkably fluid. Some airlines fold under the relentless assault of the majors, but others are eager to enter the fray. Here are some airlines that at press time had announced their intention to take off in the coming months. Perhaps by the time you read these words, some of them will be airborne.

Access Air (ZA)

(877) 462-2237
www.accessair.com

After a brief period of operating a limited route system from Des Moines, Iowa, linking Midwest communities like the Quad Cities and Peoria with New York and Los Angeles, AccessAir went into Chapter 11 bankruptcy. They are still offering charter flights while restructuring.

Cardinal Airlines

(407) 757-7388
www.cardinalairlines.com

Cardinal plans to inaugurate all-first-class service from Melbourne, FL (on the central Florida Atlantic coast) with flights to Baltimore. Eventually they hope to add Dallas, Kansas City,

Chicago, Philadelphia, Newark, and Hartford to their list of destinations. Cardinal says its first-class fares will approximate the restricted coach fares available on other airlines.

CityLink

(219) 944-3868

This completely ticketless one-class carrier hopes to operate out of Gary, IN, just 20 miles from downtown Chicago, offering 7- and 3-day advance as well as walk-up fares. CityLink's projected destinations include Newark, Dallas, Orlando, Pittsburgh, and Minneapolis. Current plans are to get airborne in March, 2001.

Crystal Airways

(863) 679-8228

Based in Tampa and looking for a first-quarter 2001 launch, Crystal is aimed at the business traveler, offering four-abreast first class seating and a single fare between city pairs that is sharply lower than unrestricted coach. Quality food service and onboard conference rooms are other components of the concept. One way fares cited on its web site include $570 from Tampa to Seattle and $300 from Tampa to Hartford.

DC Air

With leased jets from United and an apparent lock on slots at Washington's close-in Reagan National Airport, DC Air plans low-fare service to 44 cities, including Hartford, CT, and Manchester, NH.

Northern Airlines

(315) 454-3600
www.flynorthern.com

At press time, this all-coach, ticketless start-up planned to offer point-to-point service between Syracuse, NY and Boston, Newark, and Niagara Falls on Fokker F28s beginning in December of 2000. Its proposed three-step fare structure (walk-up, 7-day, and 14-day) anticipated fares ranging from $59 to $89. Another plus: free beer and wine.

Oneida Airlines

(315) 793-3366

www.flyoneida.com

Based in Utica, this well-financed new entrant hopes to bring low-fare relief to eight upstate New York cities by early 2001. Also slated for service are Boston, New York, Washington, and Chicago.

The Coast Airlines

(503) 288-8855

Initially, The Coast plans to link its hometown of Portland, OR, with New York, using Airbus aircraft. Later it hopes to add Boston and Washington.

European low-fare airlines

The same spirit of deregulation that swept America in the late seventies hit Europe nearly 20 years later. Most of the airlines listed here follow the same no-frills model as their American cousins — ticketless travel, limited in-flight services, unrestricted one way fares, and so forth. Many of them operate from lesser-known secondary airports. Only a few have U.S.-based reservations operations. Some have online booking at their web sites.

Aero Lloyd

(011) (49) 6171-625-500

www.aerolloyd.de

Flying out of its dual hubs of Frankfurt and Berlin, Aero Lloyd offers some 60 destinations as far afield as Luxor and Reykjavik. Its web site is in German but contains a route map and a helpful chart of destinations.

Air Europa

(800) 327-1225

(888) 2 EUROPA

www.globalia-corp.com/40/40.html

This Spanish airline, which flies to Madrid from New York's

JFK, has decent coverage of Spain from Madrid and Barcelona. It also flies to Paris, London, and a goodly selection of Scandinavian cities.

Air One

(011) (390) 1478 48880
www.air-one.it

Air One operates out of Milan with a frequent shuttle service to Rome and what it advertises as the lowest fares in the market to London (Stansted). It has a frequent flyer program allied with Swissair. Fares are lowest midday (11:00 a.m. to 3:00 p.m.) and on weekends.

buzz

(011) (44) 0870-240-7070
www.buzzaway.com

Part of KLM, buzz (which prefers the trendy, lower-case spelling) operates a hub from London's Stansted to such destinations as Berlin, Bordeaux, Dusseldorf, Frankfurt, Hamburg, Helsinki, Lyon, Marseille, Milan, Paris, and Vienna. buzz is a ticketless airline and penalizes those who don't book online by adding £2 to the fare (unless the buyer uses a debit card). All onboard drinks, snacks, and meals must be purchased (which can be done online prior to the flight). It costs £10 to use a Stansted "business lounge" with laptop plug ins (Internet access extra), magazines, newspapers, snacks, and drinks. There are two ticket options, Done Deals (which are always roundtrip, cannot be changed or refunded, and require flyers to stay away at least two nights or a Saturday night) and Open Deals (which allow great flexibility and are priced as one way trips). Recent Done Deal fares included Paris for between £65 and £125 and Vienna for between £95 and £150. Open Deal one way fares on the same routes were £105 to £125 and £120 to £140, respectively. buzz offers four price levels on Done Deals and three on Open Deals.

CityBird

(888) 637-4985
www.citybird.com

This Brussels-based carrier flies a limited number of flights to Brussels from Orlando and Miami, offering unrestricted one way fares. Fares are capacity controlled yielding two fare levels in business class and six in coach. Getting the lowest fare requires advance booking and careful comparison. Its fares will appeal most to business travelers on short trips. The in-house tour operation offers some attractive Brussels packages. CityBird's US-based reservationists can also book you on Virgin Express flights (see below).

Condor

(800) 524-6975
www.condor.de
Condor, based in Germany, offers an online "Fly & Savings Tariff" to selected destinations on selected dates that you can reserve online if your German is good enough.

easyJet

(011) (44) 870-6-000-000
www.easyjet.com
easyJet is a feisty little operator that has expanded from serving Scotland (out of London's Luton Airport) to serving European destinations as far afield as Athens in decidedly no-frills style with a fleet of Boeing 737-300s. Bookings can only be made directly with the airline (no travel agents). Phone bookings are accepted only for flights within two months of the booking dates. Flights farther out, which will usually have the lowest fares, can only be booked on the web site. The airline is ticketless and accepts only credit or debit cards. Fares are one way only, unrestricted, and capacity controlled with the lowest one way fares, before taxes, recently ranging between £17.50 (Aberdeen) and £37.50 (Athens).

Eurowings

(011) (49) 231 92 45 333
www.eurowings.de
Eurowings uses a single-class configuration on all it flights. Its lowest fare category, "Special Fare Restricted," applies to only

a limited number of seats per flight and carries advance purchase requirements of anywhere from 7 to 21 days.

Bookings can be made online through a somewhat cumbersome booking engine. Online booking requires immediate payment by credit card; you pick up an actual ticket prior to boarding. Eurowings offers very good coverage of major German cities, plus destinations in England, France, Switzerland, Italy, Poland, Sweden, and the Netherlands. The web site has an English version with a link to a German auction site where you can bid on Eurowings flights if you wish.

Go

(011) (44) 845-60-54321
www.go-fly.com

Go was created by British Airways in 1998 as a strictly low-fare, no-frills ticketless airline. Its routes (all from London's Stansted Airport) include Edinburgh, Copenhagen, Lisbon, Prague, and five cities in Italy — Milan, Venice, Bologna, Naples, and Rome.

It has two fare types. Standard Fares are "return only, nonrefundable, non-changeable and have a two-night minimum stay." Flexible Fares are either one way or return and can be changed or cancelled, with credit given for future travel. International one way fares have been quoted as low as £50. Fares are capacity controlled and can be booked online at Go's colorful web site.

Ryanair

(800) 365-5563
www.ryanair.ie

Using three of London's airports (Stansted, Luton, and Gatwick), this Irish carrier offers service to Ireland and to France, Italy, Norway, and Sweden. From Dublin, it flies to Brussels, Paris, and Lyon as well as to London. In the past, it has offered two-for-one deals to continental destinations for around $82 (that's $41 each!). Ryanair bills itself as "Europe's largest and most successful low fares airline" and uses a fleet of all Boeing 737s.

Spanair

(888) 545-5757
www.spanair.com

Spanair is notable for flying from Washington (Dulles) to Madrid and offering some very attractive published fares, sometimes around $300 roundtrip. Once in Spain, it offers good value on domestic flights, with roundtrips offering a better value than one ways. It also flies from Spain to Copenhagen, London, and Frankfurt but fares on these routes don't seem to be a great bargain. Its web site offers a very handy schedule and fare finder, with a built in currency converter, and bookings can be made online.

The "AirOferta" program sells leftover seats for domestic flights within the next week at fire sale prices. You can find it on the web site (in Spanish) but must call 902-131415 in Spain to purchase tickets. A recent check found roundtrips to Bilbao for $69 and to the Canary Islands for $125.

Virgin Express

(011) (44) (207) 744 0004 in the UK
(011) (32) 2-752-0505 in Brussels
www.virgin-express.com

Despite its British antecedents Virgin Express, the low-fare ticketless branch of Virgin Atlantic, uses Brussels as a hub to serve destinations in Spain, France, Italy, the Netherlands, Denmark, England, and Ireland. There is also service between both Madrid and Barcelona to Rome. Fares are based on one way travel and tend to be in the $75 to $85 range.

The fare from London Stansted to Shannon was recently less than $60. Roundtrips are not exactly twice the one way fares because of departure tax differences from place to place. You can book online and the web site occasionally offers seat auctions and special fares.

South American low-fare airlines

The savings beat goes on, this time with a Latin lilt, as the low-fare revolution spreads to South America and the Caribbean nation of Trinidad and Tobago.

Aeropostal

(888) 912-8466
www.aeropostal.com

This Venezuelan carrier links Caracas to Orlando and Miami with very competitive fares. In addition to covering Venezuela, it flies to Ecuador, Peru, and several Caribbean islands (including Cuba). It is one of the few low-fare airlines that does not offer ticketless travel.

Air Caribbean

(868) 623-2500
www.aircaribbean.com

With a hub in Port of Spain, this tiny start-up flies to Guyana, Barbados, Grenada, and Miami.

LAPA

(011) (54) 11 4114 5272
(770) 579-8373 in Atlanta
www.lapa.com.ar

In addition to many cities in Argentina, this Buenos Aires-based carrier flies to two cities in neighboring Uruguay. At press time, had announced thrice-weekly service to Atlanta for $299 one way.

Asia/Pacific low-fare airlines

Air-Do

(011) (81) 3 5350 7333
www.airdo.co.jp (in Japanese)

Ticketless Air-Do brings some fare relief to the Sapporo market, currently its only destination from Tokyo. You can book online if you read Japanese (and have the right fonts in your computer).

Freedom Air International

(011) (64) 9 912 6980
(0800) 600 500 (toll-free in New Zealand)
www.freedomair.com

Based in Auckland, this ticketless carrier covers New Zealand and also flies to Fiji and four cities in eastern Australia. It occasionally offers special fares on its web site. It has a three-tiered fare structure, with one way fares to Sydney starting at less than US$200.

Impulse Airlines

(011) (61) (02) 9317 5400
www.impulseairlines.com.au

Headquartered in Sydney, Impulse flies to 11 Australian cities. Impulse says it fares "don't come with complicated restrictions." Recently a one way ticket to Melbourne was quoted at $139 (Australian).

Skymark Airlines

(011) (81) 3 3433 6455
www.skymark.co.jp (in Japanese)

In addition to Sapporo, Skymark flies from Tokyo to Osaka and Fukuoka. In 2001, it hopes to add Korea and Guam to the list. It is completely ticketless. Online booking presents the same challenges as with Air-Do.

Chapter Five

Air Passes

Air passes, sometimes called visitor fares, can be a very shrewd way of allocating your travel dollar when traveling overseas. They are, in effect, come-ons offered by airlines (but sometimes underwritten by governments) to lure more American or European tourists with their hard currency and free-spending ways and to encourage them to visit parts of the host country they might otherwise never even hear about, let alone see.

No two air pass programs are exactly alike, so generalizing is difficult, but here goes anyway. Typically an air pass must be purchased here in the United States (or sometimes anywhere else in the world except the destination) prior to departure. Air pass programs cover anywhere from a single country to an entire continent. The program will provide you with either a true pass or a series of coupons. A true pass allows for unlimited (usually space available) travel for a specified period of time, much like the more familiar Eurailpass. Coupon programs feature booklets of tickets sold in predetermined amounts that can be exchanged for travel in the host country or region during a specified period of time.

With their buy-in-bulk discounts, air passes can often seem too good a deal to pass up. But an air pass is not always the best solution for every destination or every vacation, and using them wisely will take some forethought on the traveler's part. Do you really want to spend a week zipping all over the Hawaiian Islands? Or would it make more sense to find a great beach and just relax? On the other hand, using an air pass in vast countries like Australia and Brazil can make sense, especially if your visit is long enough to allow you to sample several different regions. Obviously, air passes will appeal more to those who like to run around seeing as much as possible in the short time allotted them during the typical American vacation and less to those who prefer to stay put. But even if you want to run around, traveling by rail, bus, or car might prove a more enjoyable and interesting experience. Truth be told, a domestic flight in Italy is much like a domestic flight anywhere; but driving the winding roads of Tuscany is an adventure that, should you survive, will be retold many times. So consider your destination and your personal travel style well before deciding on an air pass. And make sure to read all the fine print before you plunk down your money.

Most air passes can be obtained either directly from the airline or program, from a travel agent, or through a tour operator. In the case of some of the more obscure destinations, you may have to search out a travel agent or tour company that specializes in that part of the world.

Evaluating an Air Pass

Air passes vary widely in what they offer as well as in what they do and do not allow you to do. Getting clear on exactly what you're buying will not only help you make the buying decision but will also prevent any unpleasant surprises later.

- *Coupon or Pass?* Most obviously you will want to know if you are buying a pass for unlimited travel or a fixed number of coupons. If it's a pass, get clear on how you can use your pass. Is it strictly space-available? Are there advance booking requirements? If it's coupons, what precisely are the booking requirements and can you live with them? Typically a coupon will be good for all nonstop or "direct" flights (i.e. flights that stop once or twice before reaching your final destination). Once you get off one plane to board another, however, you'll most likely be using another coupon. In some cases, the pass program takes the form of a "circle trip" in which all travel from Point A to Point B to Point C and so forth, back to Point A is selected and booked at the time of purchase.

- *Eligibility.* Every pass program imposes some limits on who can buy them. The typical air pass program requires that you be a citizen or resident of some country other than the one (or ones) to which you will be traveling, that you buy your pass in your home country prior to departure, and that you fly the sponsoring airline to the foreign destination(s). There are exceptions to these rules in some programs.

- *Cost.* It's a pretty safe bet that you will be saving money over what you would spend if you bought individual tickets, but determining exactly how much you'll save can be difficult. In coupon programs, the per coupon cost tends to range between $90 and $140. Savings estimates range from 20% to 70%. One way of getting a sense of how much you'll save is to price individual trips either with the airline or on an Internet booking engine (if it has one!). Of course this won't always give you an accurate reading since sometimes the cost of a ticket bought in the U.S. can vary widely from the cost of a ticket purchased abroad. Note, too, any planned trips that will require using two coupons, thus doubling the cost.

  Airport, departure, and other taxes are usually additional and collected at the time of the flight. Depending on the location and the program, taxes can add as much as 37% to the effective cost of a flight.

  Cost can also be affected by other factors. Many programs require that you fly into the country or region on a specific airline in order to qualify for the pass. Others will let you fly another airline but charge more for the pass if you do. When you fly can also affect the cost (see Seasonality, below). Many air pass programs offer discounts for children, with the term "child" generally being defined more generously than it usually is by domestic American airlines.

  By the way, prices quoted below were accurate at

press time, but fares do change, mostly upward, so double-check before making firm travel plans.

- *Coupon minimums and maximums.* In coupon programs it is pretty typical to find a minimum purchase requirement of three or four coupons. Beyond the minimum, coupons can usually be purchased separately. These additional coupons usually cost more, on a per coupon basis, than the ones purchased to satisfy the minimum. Eight coupons seems to be a fairly typical maximum but programs vary, from a minimum of one to no maximum at all, so check. Be careful! Overbuying is easy to do, just like piling your plate too high at the buffet table. Make sure you'll actually have time to use all those coupons. Remember that in some countries, the on-time record of the local airline may leave something to be desired. Typically, coupons are nontransferable, that is, the same person must use all the coupons in a book.

- *Destinations offered.* Many programs let you fly anywhere on the participating airline's route system, but others limit destinations or charge more for travel to some regions of the country or continent. Some programs issue different passes for different regions.

- *Time limit.* Air pass programs are all time-limited in some way, anywhere from a week to three months. In some cases the time limit is affected by how many coupons you buy, in other cases you can buy more time if you wish.

- *Seasonality.* Some air passes are valid only at certain times of the year. Others vary in cost between low season and high season (and, sometimes, shoulder season). Just what constitutes low and high seasons will change from destination to destination.

- *Flexibility.* In my opinion, the more flexibility a pass offers the better. Some programs require you to decide where and when you'll be traveling before you leave home, others offer total freedom (subject to space availability). Some programs have advance booking requirements and penalties for making changes. Some programs limit how often you can travel to the same city. A series of open jaw trips may make more sense (and be more economical) than constantly flying back to a central hub. You can add additional flexibility by flying back from a different city from the one in which you landed, if the airline permits this.

- *Safety.* Many air passes are just like cash. Lose it and it's gone, no refund, no recourse. Some programs have refund policies in place. Consider insurance, which is offered at an extra cost by some programs. In any event, understand that you will have to take very good care of your pass or coupons.

With that in mind, let's turn our attention to the bounty of air pass programs seeking to lure you to their corner of the world. First a caveat: Like so much in air travel, the air pass scene is extremely fluid, so don't hold it against me if some of these deals have evaporated by the time you read this. Of course there's always hope that an airline that has ended an air pass promotion will revive it next year.

About the listings

The goal of these listings is to call to your attention programs that might be appealing and highlight their salient features. However, I cannot answer all your questions, so you will have to get in touch and do your research. I have tried to list the most logical point of contact for further information and tickets; this is not always the sponsoring airline. You will probably find that reservations personnel are not necessarily up to speed on their airline's pass programs. You will generally do better to request a brochure so you can examine the fine print at your leisure. As always, a knowledgeable travel agent, who specializes in the destination you are considering, will be an invaluable asset and won't cost you any more money.

I have also provided airline web sites, even though many of them do not carry information about their airline's air pass program, and when they do it tends to be incomplete. It's a logical place to look, though, and the information might appear at some point in the future. Rather than try to provide the specific addresses (or URLs) for pages buried deep within a web site, which are lengthy and subject to frequent change, I have provided the home page address. Any web site worth its salt should make it relatively easy to find the information you're looking for. (Although, Lord knows, too many do not.)

I have arranged these listings geographically by continent or region of the globe. Under each geographical heading, I have listed the air pass programs alphabetically by the name of the pass, since many programs involve multiple airlines and/or multiple countries. It should be fairly easy to scan the list for the countries and regions that most interest you.

Europe

Since Europe is the most popular foreign vacation destination for Americans, after Mexico and the Caribbean, it's not too surprising that a wide variety of air pass programs are seeking to grab a larger share of that tourist market. For many people, myself included, the best way to see Europe is on the ground. However, many of the passes listed here allow you to fly considerable distances, making for some highly creative vacation itineraries.

Discover Europe

British Midland
(800) 788-0555
www.iflybritishmidland.com

> *Type:* Coupons.
> *Eligibility:* Non-European residents; fly in on any airline.
> *Cost:* $109 or $159 depending on distance from London.
> *Min/Max:* No minimum or maximum.
> *Destinations:* 25 destinations.
> *Time limit:* Three months from commencement of travel.
> *Flexibility:* Book first flight and rest remain open.
> *Comments:* All flights to and from London hub; best for open jaw trips.

Discover Europe Coupons

Lufthansa
(800) 645-3880
www.lufthansa-usa.com

Type: Coupons.

Eligibility: Purchase in U.S. and fly in on any airline; but if a carrier other than Lufthansa is used, European travel must begin in Frankfurt.

Cost: $119 to $159 for first three coupons; youth coupons $99 to $139.

Min/Max: Minimum of three stops, maximum of 12.

Destinations: Lufthansa destinations in Europe only.

Time limit: Determined by transatlantic ticket, up to a year.

Seasonality: Valid all year; high season is May through September.

Comments: A similar program is available from Canada.

Easy Spain

Air Europa
(888) 238-7672
www.easyspain.com

Type: Coupons.

Eligibility: Purchase coupons from TravelPlan USA and fly in on an Air Europa flight from New York's JFK.

Cost: $60 to $90 per coupon, depending on season and other factors.

Min/Max: No minimum or maximum.

Destinations: One coupon for domestic flights, two coupons for destinations outside Spain.

Time limit: One year.

Flexibility: Reserve ahead or use coupons on a space available basis.

Comments: Coupons can also be used for hotel stays and rental cars.

Euro Flyer Pass

Air France
(800) 237-2747
www.airfrance.com
> *Type:* Coupons.
> *Eligibility:* Purchase in U.S., fly in on any airline, begin travel in Paris.
> *Cost:* $99 to $120 per coupon, depending on season.
> *Min/Max:* Minimum of three, maximum of nine.
> *Destinations:* More than 20 European destinations.
> *Time limit:* Two months.
> *Seasonality:* Valid all year; high season is April to October.
> *Flexibility:* Prebook first segment. Open jaws permitted.

Eurofares

Lufthansa
(800) 645-3880
www.lufthansa-usa.com
> *Type:* Coupons.
> *Eligibility:* Purchase in U.S. and fly in on Lufthansa.
> *Cost:* $89 per segment.
> *Min/Max:* No minimum, maximum of six.
> *Destinations:* Lufthansa destinations in Europe only.
> *Time limit:* Valid for length of season.
> *Seasonality:* January through mid June.
> *Flexibility:* Book all segments in advance.

EuroGreensaver Pass

Aer Lingus
(800) 474-7424
www.aerlingus.ie
> *Type:* Coupons.
> *Eligibility:* For U.S. passengers in conjunction with transatlantic travel on Aer Lingus.
> *Cost:* $60 to $99 per coupon.
> *Min/Max:* Minimum of two, maximum of six.
> *Destinations:* Cities in Ireland, the UK, and Europe.

Time limit: Length of season.

Seasonality: Winter.

Flexibility: Must reserve first segment prior to departure; cannot travel any segment more than once in same direction.

Comments: $99 coupons are for travel to continental destinations.

EuroPass

Iberia

(800) 772-4642

www.iberia.com

Type: Coupons.

Eligibility: Purchase in U.S. in conjunction with transatlantic travel on Iberia.

Cost: $125 or $155 per coupon.

Min/Max: Minimum of two, no maximum.

Destinations: European and some Mideastern destinations.

Time limit: Three months from commencement of travel.

Seasonality: Valid all year.

Flexibility: Must prebook first segment. No standby allowed. No limit on number of times a destination may be visited. No rerouting.

Comments: $155 coupons are for one way travel to Cairo and Tel Aviv.

Europe Airpass

British Airways

(800) 247-9297

www.us.british-airways.com

Type: Coupons.

Eligibility: Purchase in U.S., fly in on any airline.

Cost: $92 or $185 per segment, depending on distance.

Min/Max: Minimum of three, maximum of 12.

Destinations: British Airways' European destinations as far east as Moscow and Baku in Azerbaijan.

Time limit: Three months from commencement of travel.

Seasonality: Valid all year.

Flexibility: Must prebook all travel seven days prior to arrival in UK.

EuropeByAir.com Flight Pass

Sixteen smaller European airlines
(888) 387-2479
www.europebyair.com

> *Type:* Coupons.
> *Eligibility:* Must be a citizen or permanent resident of the U.S. or Canada. Buy in U.S. or Europe. Fly any airline to Europe.
> *Cost:* $99 per coupon. Taxes can be hefty on some departures.
> *Min/Max:* No minimum, no maximum.
> *Destinations:* 130 cities in 26 countries.
> *Time limit:* 120 days from date you specify when ordering.
> *Seasonality:* Valid all year.
> *Flexibility:* Valid on non-stops only. Reservations can be made in the U.S. or Europe; book 24 hours prior to flight time or fly standby.
> *Comments:* The mother of all European air passes lets you travel from the Canary Islands to Moscow and from Shannon to Crete.

Europlus Air Pass

Alitalia
(800) 223-5730
www.alitaliausa.com

> *Type:* Coupons.
> *Eligibility:* Purchase in U.S. in conjunction with transatlantic travel on Alitalia.
> *Cost:* $299 for three, $100 each additional.
> *Min/Max:* Minimum of three, no maximum.
> *Destinations:* All Alitalia destinations in Europe.
> *Time limit:* One year.
> *Seasonality:* Valid all year.
> *Flexibility:* Must prebook first segment. Segments must be booked at least two weeks in advance; no standby.

Hungarian Pass to Europe

Malev
(800) 223-6884
www.malev.hu

> *Type:* Coupons.
> *Eligibility:* Purchase in U.S. and fly Malev to Budapest.
> *Cost:* Three for $330 or $420; $90 or $110 additional depending on season.
> *Min/Max:* Minimum of three, maximum of nine.
> *Destinations:* Malev's European destinations.
> *Time limit:* Up to a year.
> *Seasonality:* Valid all year; high season is May 20 to October 31.
> *Flexibility:* Must prebook first segment, rest can be open. Standby permitted.

Passport to Europe

Northwest and KLM
(800) 374-7747
www.nwa.com

> *Type:* Coupons.
> *Eligibility:* Must purchase in U.S. and fly on Northwest or KLM.
> *Cost:* $100 per coupon.
> *Min/Max:* Minimum of three, maximum of 12.
> *Destinations:* More than 90 European cities.
> *Time limit:* Determined by dates of transatlantic ticket.
> *Seasonality:* Valid all year.
> *Flexibility:* Plan your itinerary before leaving the U.S. You can purchase additional coupons in Europe.

Spain Pass

Spanair
(888) 545-5757
www.spanair.com

> *Type:* Coupons.
> *Eligibility:* Nonresidents of Spain in conjunction with an

international ticket.

Cost: $195 for three, $240 for four, $295 for five, $345 for six, $395 for seven, $445 for eight.

Min/Max: Three coupon minimum, eight maximum.

Destinations: All destinations in Spain.

Time limit: 90 days.

Seasonality: Valid all year.

Flexibility: Reservation for first segment must be made before arrival.

Comments: A pass that includes the Canary Islands has a higher per coupon price.

Visit Baltic Pass

SAS
(800) 221-2350
www.flysas.com

Type: Coupons.

Eligibility: Purchase in U.S. in conjunction with transatlantic travel on SAS.

Cost: $105 each.

Min/Max: No minimum, maximum of four.

Destinations: For travel between Denmark, Norway, Sweden, Finland, parts of Russia, and the Baltic states.

Time limit: Three months.

Seasonality: Valid all year.

Flexibility: Some routing restrictions.

Visit Europe Air Pass

SAS and British Midland
(800) 221-2350
www.flysas.com

Type: Coupons.

Eligibility: Purchase in U.S. in conjunction with transatlantic travel on SAS.

Cost: $105 to $225 depending on route.

Min/Max: Minimum of one, maximum of five.

Destinations: For travel between Copenhagen, Oslo, and Stockholm; between Scandinavia and all SAS Euro-

pean destinations; and on British Midland flights.
Time limit: Three months.
Seasonality: Valid all year.
Flexibility: Some routing restrictions.

Visit Europe Fares

Austrian Airlines
(800) 843-0002
www.austrianair.com
> *Type:* Coupons.
> *Eligibility:* Purchase in U.S. and fly to Vienna from New York, Washington, or Atlanta.
> *Cost:* $299 for three, $389 for four, $469 for five, $539 for six.
> *Min/Max:* Minimum of three, maximum of six.
> *Destinations:* Anywhere in Europe on route systems of Austrian Airlines, Tyrolean Airways, or Lauda.
> *Time limit:* 60 days.
> *Flexibility:* Must book at least first flight.

Visit Norway

Braathens SAFE
(800) 722-4126
nettvik.no/terminalen/braathens/
> *Type:* Coupons.
> *Eligibility:* Purchase in U.S., fly to Norway on any airline.
> *Cost:* $85 per "segment."
> *Min/Max:* No minimum or maximum.
> *Destinations:* Domestic Norway only.
> *Time limit:* Length of season.
> *Seasonality:* May to September.
> *Flexibility:* Book and confirm all flights before departure.
> *Comments:* Some flights require two or three "segments."

Visit Scandinavia

SAS
(800) 221-2350
www.flysas.com

Type: Coupons.

Eligibility: Purchase in U.S. in conjunction with transatlantic travel on SAS.

Cost: $75 to $225 depending on route.

Min/Max: Minimum of one, maximum of eight.

Destinations: For travel in and between Denmark, Norway, and Sweden; also between Sweden and Finland.

Time limit: Three months.

Seasonality: Valid all year.

Flexibility: Some routing restrictions.

Visit Spain

Iberia
(800) 772-4642
www.iberia.com

Type: Coupons.

Eligibility: Purchase in U.S. in conjunction with transatlantic travel on Iberia.

Cost: $260 to $349 for four, $50 each additional.

Min/Max: Minimum of four, no maximum.

Destinations: Iberia's domestic destinations (excluding the Canaries).

Time limit: None.

Seasonality: Valid all year. Higher rates during high season, from mid-June through September.

Flexibility: Must prebook first segment. No standby allowed.

Comments: For a pass that includes the Canary Islands, the cost is $299 or $349 for four coupons.

Latin America

Air Touring Pass

Avensa and Servivensa
(800) 428-3672
www.avensa.com.ve

Type: Coupons.

Eligibility: Must be purchased in any region except Latin America and the Caribbean.

Cost: $55 to $200 per coupon, depending on destination.

Min/Max: Minimum of four, no maximum specified.

Destinations: Venezuela, Aruba, Curaçao, Colombia, Peru, Panama, and Mexico.

Time limit: 45 days.

Seasonality: Valid all year.

Flexibility: Cannot fly any route twice in the same direction.

Brazil Air Pass

Varig, VASP, and Transbrasil
(800) 468-2744
www.varig.com.br

Type: Coupons.

Eligibility: Purchase in U.S., fly in on qualifying airline.

Cost: $290, $350, $490, or $540 depending on region.

Min/Max: Minimum of four or five; additional coupons $100 in some regions.

Destinations: Varies with region, all within Brazil.

Time limit: 21 days from when you use the first coupon.

Seasonality: All year, but costs more in December, February, June, and July.

Flexibility: Flights must be booked and confirmed for entire itinerary.

Discover Colombia

Avianca
(800) 284-2622

Type: Coupons.

Eligibility: Purchase in U.S. in conjunction with international travel on Avianca. If you fly a different airline, cost of pass goes up.

Cost: $100 or $119 for three, $200 or $290 for five.

Min/Max: Minimum of three, maximum of five.

Destinations: Domestic destinations only.

Time limit: 30 days.

> *Seasonality:* Higher fares apply to high season, June through August and December.
>
> *Flexibility:* Must pick destinations in advance but can leave dates open.
>
> *Comments:* Visits to San Andres and Leticia cost extra.

LABPass

Lloyd Aero Boliviano
(800) 327-7407
labairlines.bo.net

> *Type:* Coupons.
>
> *Eligibility:* Purchase in U.S. and fly in on LAB; if you fly in on another carrier, pass costs $250.
>
> *Cost:* $200 for your choice of four cities.
>
> *Destinations:* Six cities in Bolivia.
>
> *Time limit:* 30 days.
>
> *Seasonality:* Valid all year.
>
> *Flexibility:* Can only visit each city once, except to make a connection. Must book and confirm all travel at the same time.

Maya Pass

Aviateca, Lacsa, and Taca
(800) 327-9832
www.grupotaca.com

> *Type:* Coupons.
>
> *Eligibility:* Purchase outside region in conjunction with a flight into the region.
>
> *Cost:* Priced by itinerary; receive a discount if you fly in on one of the sponsoring airlines.
>
> *Min/Max:* Minimum of four, no maximum.
>
> *Destinations:* Eleven cities in Mexico, Belize, Guatemala, El Salvador, and Honduras (the "Mundo Maya").
>
> *Time limit:* 60 days.
>
> *Seasonality:* Valid all year.
>
> *Flexibility:* Must reserve three days before any departure; no standby allowed. Short stopovers (less than 24 hours) are permitted to make a connection.

Comments: This pass will give you access to all the major Mayan ruin sites.

MercoSur AirPass

Varig, Aerolineas Argentinas, and LanChile
(800) 333-0276

> *Type:* Coupons.
> *Eligibility:* Purchase in U.S. in conjunction with an international flight, which must be on one of the sponsoring airlines.
> *Cost:* $225 to $870 per segment, depending on distance flown.
> *Min/Max:* Visit a minimum of three countries, a maximum of four (or a maximum of eight coupons total and four per country).
> *Destinations:* Cities in Argentina, Brazil, Chile, Paraguay, and Uruguay.
> *Time limit:* 30 days.
> *Seasonality:* Valid all year.
> *Flexibility:* Open jaw and circle trips allowed.
> *Comments:* Itinerary must be picked prior to departure. Plan carefully to minimize distances flown between cities.

Visit Argentina Pass

Aerolineas Argentinas or Austral
(800) 333-0276
www.aerolineas.com

> *Type:* Coupons.
> *Eligibility:* Non-Argentineans residing abroad; fly in on any airline.
> *Cost:* $339 for three, $105 each additional.
> *Min/Max:* Minimum of three, maximum of eight.
> *Destinations:* Major cities within Argentina.
> *Time limit:* 30 days.
> *Seasonality:* All year.
> *Flexibility:* Must pre-book all travel; date changes are free but only one free rerouting is allowed.

Visit Central America

Taca, Aviateca, Lacsa, and Nica.
(800) 327-9832
www.grupotaca.com

> *Type:* Coupons.
> *Eligibility:* Purchase outside region in conjunction with a flight into the region from a qualifying city.
> *Cost:* Priced by itinerary.
> *Min/Max:* Minimum of two destinations, maximum of ten.
> *Destinations:* Eleven cities in Nicaragua, Belize, Guatemala, El Salvador, and Honduras (the "Mundo Maya").
> *Time limit:* 60 days.
> *Seasonality:* Valid all year; high season is July, August, November, and December.
> *Flexibility:* Must reserve 21 days before any departure; no standby allowed. Short stopovers (less than 24 hours) are permitted when necessary to make a connection.

Visit Chile Pass

LanChile
(800) 735-5526
www.lanchile.com

> *Type:* Coupons.
> *Eligibility:* Purchase abroad in conjunction with international travel on LanChile.
> *Cost:* $250 for three, $60 each additional.
> *Min/Max:* Minimum of three, maximum of six.
> *Destinations:* Various "packages" of cities offered.
> *Time limit:* None.
> *Seasonality:* Valid all year.
> *Comments:* Other passes available.

Caribbean

Caribbean Airpass

BWIA International Airways
(800) 538-2942
www.bwee.com
> *Type:* Pass.
> *Eligibility:* Must be purchased in conjunction with a flight from Europe or U.S.
> *Cost:* $449.
> *Destinations:* 13 destinations.
> *Time limit:* 30 days.
> *Seasonality:* All year, except the Christmas to New Year period.
> *Flexibility:* Cannot visit the same island twice except to make a connection.

Super Caribbean Explorer

Liat
(268) 462-0700 (Note: This phone number is in Antigua.)
> *Type:* Pass.
> *Eligibility:* Purchase in U.S. or in the Caribbean.
> *Cost:* $475.
> *Min/Max:* Minimum of two segments, no maximum.
> *Destinations:* Everywhere LIAT flies from Puerto Rico to Guyana, about 25 destinations.
> *Time limit:* 30 days.
> *Seasonality:* Valid all year.
> *Flexibility:* Book and confirm all segments in advance; $35 penalty for date changes. Can only visit same airport once, except to make connections.
> *Comments:* This pass works best if you use an open jaw ticket for your travel to and from the area.

Asia

All Asia Pass

Cathay Pacific
(800) 233-2742
www.cathay-usa.com

> *Type:* Pass.
> *Eligibility:* U.S. residents with U.S. mailing addresses; 30-day advance purchase.
> *Cost:* $1,099, including air from New York, Los Angeles, or San Francisco.
> *Destinations:* Hong Kong plus 15 cities from Bali to Tokyo.
> *Time limit:* 30 days from arrival in Hong Kong.
> *Seasonality:* Most of the year, although the price goes up $200 for summer travel and $50 one way for weekend departures from the U.S.
> *Flexibility:* You can purchase additional cities and time, up to 60 days.
> *Comments:* The mother of all Asian air passes and one of the best deals in the air.

Amazing Thailand Fares

Thai Airways
(800) 426-5204
www.thaiairways.com

> *Type:* Coupons.
> *Eligibility:* Purchase outside Thailand in conjunction with air travel on any airline.
> *Cost:* $199 for four, $49 each additional.
> *Min/Max:* Minimum of four, maximum of eight.
> *Destinations:* Domestic destinations only.
> *Time limit:* Three months.
> *Seasonality:* Valid all year.

ASEAN Circle Trip Fares

Thai Airways and others
(800) 426-5204

www.thaiairways.com

> *Type:* Coupons.
>
> *Eligibility:* Purchase outside Thailand in conjunction with air travel on any airline.
>
> *Cost:* $297 for three, $396 for four, $495 for five, and $594 for six stopovers.
>
> *Min/Max:* Minimum of two, maximum of six.
>
> *Destinations:* Thailand, Brunei, Indonesia, Malaysia, Philippines, Singapore, and Vietnam.
>
> *Time limit:* Two months.
>
> *Seasonality:* Valid all year.
>
> *Flexibility:* Travel must be to two, three, or four ASEAN countries depending on pass purchased.

Discover India

Indian Airlines

(800) 957-3299; (212) 997-3300

www.nic.in/indian-airlines/

> *Type:* Pass.
>
> *Eligibility:* Purchase in U.S. in conjunction with your flight to India.
>
> *Cost:* $300 for 7 days, $500 for 15 days, $750 for 21 days.
>
> *Destinations:* All destinations within India.
>
> *Time limit:* 7 to 21 days.
>
> *Seasonality:* All year.
>
> *Flexibility:* No city can be visited more than once except to transfer or connect.

Discover Malaysia Pass

Malaysia Airlines

(800) 552-9264

www.malaysiaairlines.com

> *Type:* Coupons.
>
> *Eligibility:* Purchase in U.S. or within 14 days after arrival in Malaysia, but in connection with an international flight on Malaysia Airlines.
>
> *Cost:* Five coupons for $99 for travel on the main peninsula only; if you want to include travel to Sarawak and

Sabah, the cost is $199.
Min/Max: Five coupons only.
Destinations: Domestic destinations only.
Time limit: 28 days from start of travel on the pass.
Seasonality: Valid all year.
Flexibility: Flights must be booked in advance.

India Wonder Fares

Indian Airlines
(800) 957-3299; (212) 997-3300
www.nic.in/indian-airlines/
Type: Pass.
Eligibility: Purchase in U.S. in conjunction with your
flight to India.
Cost: $300.
Destinations: Choose from four regions within India.
Time limit: One week.
Seasonality: All year.

Visit Indonesia Decade Pass

Garuda
(800) 876-2254
www.garudausa.com
Type: Circle trip.
Eligibility: Purchase in U.S. in conjunction with interna-
tional travel on any airline, but $50 surcharge applies if
carrier is not Garuda.
Cost: $330 for three cities, $550 for five, $110 each addi-
tional.
Min/Max: Visit a minimum of three cities, maximum of
eight.
Destinations: Garuda domestic destinations only.
Time limit: 60 days.
Seasonality: Valid all year.
Flexibility: Must select and book cities in advance.

Visit the Philippines

Philippine Airlines

(800) 435-9725
www.philippineair.com

>   *Type:* Coupons.
>
>   *Eligibility:* Purchase in U.S. and arrive in Manila on Philippine Airlines.
>
>   *Cost:* $180 for four, $210 for five or six, $230 for seven or eight.
>
>   *Min/Max:* Minimum of four, maximum of eight.
>
>   *Destinations:* Domestic destinations only.
>
>   *Time limit:* Length of the international ticket.
>
>   *Seasonality:* Valid all year.
>
>   *Flexibility:* Must be ticketed when purchasing international ticket, but dates can be left open.

Welcome to Japan

Japan Airlines (JAL)
(800) 525-3663
www.japanair.com

>   *Type:* Coupons.
>
>   *Eligibility:* Must purchase in U.S. but can fly to Japan on any airline.
>
>   *Cost:* ¥24,000 for two, ¥12,000 each additional.
>
>   *Min/Max:* Minimum of two, maximum of five.
>
>   *Destinations:* Anywhere in Japan.
>
>   *Time limit:* Two months.
>
>   *Seasonality:* Valid all year.
>
>   *Flexibility:* Must prebook all segments; no changes allowed on first segment, date changes only on all other segments.

Australia, New Zealand and the Pacific

Adventure Pass

Air Niugini
(949) 752-5440
www.airniugini.com.pg

>   *Type:* Coupons.

Eligibility: Purchase in North America; enter and depart
   on Air Niugini.
Cost: Four coupons for $299, $75 each additional.
Min/Max: Minimum of four, no maximum.
Destinations: Domestic New Guinea destinations only.
Time limit: 30 days.
Seasonality: Valid all year.
Flexibility: Book and confirm all flights in advance; can
   change dates but not routing.
Comments: Unused coupons are not refundable.

Aloha Island Pass

Aloha Airlines
(800) 367-5250
www.alohaair.com
Type: Pass.
Eligibility: Open to nonresidents of Hawaii; fly in on any
   airline.
Cost: $321.
Destinations: Anywhere Aloha flies.
Time limit: Seven days from the date you pick up your
   pass.
Seasonality: Valid all year.
Flexibility: Advance reservations permitted but not re-
   quired; standby travel also allowed.

Boomerang Pass

Qantas and Ansett Airlines
(800) 227-4500
www.qantas.com
Type: Coupon.
Eligibility: Purchase in U.S. in conjunction with interna-
   tional travel.
Cost: $155 to $190 per coupon depending on city pairs.
Min/Max: Minimum of two, maximum of ten.
Destinations: Australia and New Zealand.
Time limit: Valid for length of international ticket.
Seasonality: Valid all year.

Flexibility: City pairs must be specified but dates, except for first segment, can be left open. Same day connections within Australia will be considered one flight.

Comments: Once travel has commenced, coupons three through ten are fully refundable.

Discover Fiji Pass

Air Fiji
(877) 247-3454
www.airfiji.net

Type: Coupons.

Eligibility: Purchase outside Fiji only; proof of residence required on all flights. Fly in on any airline.

Cost: $270 for four.

Min/Max: Minimum of four, no maximum.

Destinations: All destinations in Fiji.

Time limit: 30 days, no extensions.

Seasonality: Valid all year.

Flexibility: Must reserve ahead; can change dates (but not routings) without penalty. Full and partial refunds possible depending on circumstances.

Explore New Zealand

Air New Zealand
(800) 262-1234
www.airnz.com

Type: Coupons.

Eligibility: Purchase abroad by nonresidents in conjunction with travel to New Zealand on any airline.

Cost: NZ$515 for three; NZ$172 for each additional.

Min/Max: Minimum of three, maximum of eight.

Destinations: All inland flights on Air New Zealand and Mt. Cook Airlines.

Time limit: None.

Seasonality: Valid all year.

Flexibility: Route must be determined in advance, dates can be left open.

G'Day Pass

Ansett
(888) 426-7388
www.ansett.com.au

> *Type:* Coupons.
> *Eligibility:* Purchase in North America and arrive on any airline.
> *Cost:* $155, $195, or $350 per segment based on zones.
> *Min/Max:* Minimum of two, maximum of ten.
> *Destinations:* New Zealand and Australia.
> *Time limit:* Validity of international ticket.
> *Seasonality:* Valid all year.
> *Flexibility:* Book all segments prior to arrival in Australia; additional segments may be purchased there.
> *Comments:* Limited seat availability. You can get better availability by paying a higher per segment fare. This pass works best if you fly into one country and back from the other (open jaw).

PolyPass

Polynesian Airlines
(800) 644-7659
www.polynesianairlines.co.nz

> *Type:* Pass.
> *Eligibility:* Must purchase in U.S.
> *Cost:* From $999.
> *Destinations:* Covers Samoa, Fiji, Tonga, Australia, New Zealand, and Pago Pago.
> *Time limit:* 45 days.
> *Seasonality:* Valid all year, except Christmas–New Year holiday.
> *Flexibility:* Unlimited travel on Polynesian Airlines; limited travel on its partner airlines.

Visit South Pacific Air Pass

Air Niugini
(949) 752-5440

www.airniugini.com.pg
> *Type:* Coupons.
> *Eligibility:* Purchase in North America.
> *Cost:* $220 per segment.
> *Min/Max:* Minimum of two, no maximum.
> *Destinations:* New Guinea and Australia.
> *Time limit:* Three months.
> *Seasonality:* Valid all year.
> *Flexibility:* Book and confirm all segments in advance; $75 penalty for changes.
> *Comments:* Begin travel in Cairns or Brisbane; requires two coupons to enter and leave New Guinea.

Visit The South Pacific Pass

Air Promotion Systems
(310) 670-7302
www.pacificislands.com
> *Type:* Coupons.
> *Eligibility:* Purchase in U.S.
> *Cost:* $175, $220, or $320 per segment, depending on distance flown.
> *Min/Max:* Minimum of two segments, no maximum.
> *Destinations:* Most of the South Pacific, including Australia, New Zealand, Fiji, Tahiti, Samoa, Guam, and the Gilbert and Solomon Islands. Uses a variety of airlines.
> *Time limit:* Six months.
> *Seasonality:* Valid all year.
> *Flexibility:* Prebooking of all segments highly recommended due to infrequency and high load factors of many of the flights.
> *Comments:* The company that sells this pass also offers a number of other South Pacific passes covering individual countries and island groups, including Discover Samoa Pass, Discover Solomons Pass, Discover Fiji Pass, Discover Vanuatu Pass, Discover Cook Islands Pass, and Discover New Caledonia Pass.

Africa

African Explorer

South African Airways
(800) 722-9675
www.saa-usa.com

> *Type:* Coupons.
> *Eligibility:* Purchase in U.S. or South Africa, but must show an international ticket on South African Airways.
> *Cost:* $70 to $150 per segment, within South Africa, up to $300 for flights outside.
> *Min/Max:* Minimum of four segments, maximum of eight.
> *Destinations:* All South African destinations and select African destinations including Nairobi and Lagos.
> *Time limit:* 60 days.
> *Seasonality:* Valid all year.
> *Flexibility:* Must book all segments at time of purchase.
> *Comments:* Most flights are out of Johannesburg, some from Capetown.

Travel Pass

Air Namibia
(212) 290-2591
www.airnamibia.com.na

> *Type:* Coupons.
> *Eligibility:* Purchase abroad or in Namibia, in conjunction with travel on Air Namibia from London or Frankfurt.
> *Cost:* $146 for two, $109 each additional.
> *Min/Max:* Minimum of two, maximum of five.
> *Destinations:* All Air Namibia destinations in Namibia, Botswana, and South Africa.
> *Time limit:* 45 days.
> *Seasonality:* Valid all year.
> *Flexibility:* Must book all segments at time of purchase. Open jaws permitted.

Chapter Six

Consolidators

So far we have discovered various ways to get the best fare through booking ploys, rebates, discounts, frequent flyer deals, or air passes. But all the strategies discussed thus far have one thing in common: you (or your travel agent) are ultimately getting the ticket from the airline itself at what is more or less "the going rate." In other words, the deals we have been examining are all available on the "open market." The airlines openly acknowledge them.

But there is another, parallel, hidden market in airline tickets that the airlines don't officially recognize, even though they are active participants in it. This is the market of consolidator tickets, which has grown up over the years due to a number of factors. Here in the United States, airline fares are deregulated and, despite what curmudgeons like me persist in seeing as price-fixing behavior on the part of the major airlines, fares on the big airlines have reached a "fair market value." And there are enough low-fare carriers serving the budget traveler to prevent any real need for a black market in airline tickets. The same is not true in most of the rest of the world where the International Air Transport Association (IATA), to which the vast majority of airlines belong, has long insisted on maintaining air fares at artificially high levels. The result: a crying need for a black, or at least gray, market. Many airlines, knowing that they will never sell all their seats at the official price, have looked to middlemen — consolidators — to help them quietly unload their excess inventory.

That's why consolidator tickets are primarily an international phenomenon. There are a number of agencies that sell discounted domestic tickets in the United States, but these are usually special situations, such as TWA, or barter deals with smaller airlines. I suspect that as the major airlines succeed in driving retail travel agents out of business they may discover a need to turn to consolidators, but for now at least, you will be looking to consolidators mainly for those overseas trips.

What is a consolidator?

In the simplest terms, a consolidator is someone who buys airplane seats wholesale and sells below retail. There is a great deal of confusion about what the term means, even within the industry, however, so perhaps we should refine our definitions somewhat, to cover the entire spectrum of those who deal in below-retail airline tickets. Definitions can get a bit slippery and there are many permutations and combinations, so hang on.

Wholesale consolidators

These are companies that specialize in cutting bulk deals with airlines and then marketing those seats, not to the general public, but to travel agencies that mark up the ticket and sell it to the ultimate consumer. These companies are probably consolidators in the truest sense.

Retail consolidators or "bucket shops"

These are companies that make bulk deals with airlines and then sell directly to the public. Or they may be travel agencies that have negotiated extremely high commissions from one or more airlines and then price the tickets they sell in such a way that they are, in effect, rebating a large portion of that commission to the traveler. They might sell tickets to travel agencies as well. Sometimes they will sell tickets to travel agents at a lower fare (called a "net fare") than the one they charge to the public. Sometimes they will sell to the public and to travel agents at the same fare, but then grant the travel agent a commission. Sometimes they will sell to both travel agents and the general public at exactly the same prices; the travel agent, of course, can mark up the ticket he or she purchased. As I use the term, a retail consolidator does little or no business apart from selling the tickets it purchases under contract from the airlines. In other words, retail consolidators are not travel agencies in the generally understood meaning of the term, even though they may have (in fact, usually do have) travel agency accreditation.

These agencies are often called "bucket shops," a British slang term that is now used pretty much worldwide. Some companies in this category disdain the bucket shop label and prefer terms like "bulk fare operator" or "discounter."

Discount travel agencies

Most dealers in consolidator tickets fall into this category. A "discount travel agency" differs from a bucket shop to the extent that it offers other travel products and services besides cheap airline tickets. It differs from a "full-service travel agency" only to the extent that it positions itself in the marketplace as a source of cheap (or cheaper) travel. These travel agencies can get their consolidator tickets in one of two ways: They can negotiate a contract with an airline or airlines, in which case they would be retail consolidators. For example, they may be tour operators on a small scale and thus have a special relationship with the airlines serving their tour destinations. Or they can purchase consolidator tickets on an as needed basis from a wholesale or retail consolidator, in which case they are simply functioning as a middleman. Discount travel agencies by their very nature sell a lot of consolidator tickets. None of this is to suggest, however, that you cannot get a consolidator ticket through a full-service travel agency. Any travel agency can get you a consolidator ticket, although a good many may choose not to do so.

Charter operators

This is another, separate category of discount travel provider which is often confused with a consolidator. Sometimes agencies that deal in consolidator tickets also deal with charter flights. Often times a charter operator is involved solely in chartering planes, usually to a single destination or a limited number of destinations. Some discount travel agencies or bucket shops may be selling charter flights, either their own or someone else's.

A major and very important difference between consolidator tickets and charter tickets is that consolidator tickets are for seats on regularly scheduled airlines. Charter tickets, in contrast, are for seats on a single flight of a single aircraft. If the charter operator can't sell enough seats on the flight, it may fold, leaving you holding a worthless ticket. If there is a mechanical problem on the chartered plane, you will sit and wait until it's fixed. That's not to say that a charter cannot be a good budget travel strategy. Just know what you're getting into before turning over your hard-earned money.

Sorting it all out

Many times it's hard to know exactly which type of operation you're dealing with. In most cases, it's not important; the result is the same — a cheap ticket. However, sometimes whom you are dealing with can make a difference.

- If you are dealing with a retail consolidator or bucket shop, you may get a better deal than you would from a discount agency that is purchasing your ticket from another source. (Then, again, you may not. It's hard to know for sure.)
- On the other hand, a discount travel agency may have more to offer in terms of service and hand-holding. Many consolidators have more in common with old world bazaars, where customer service is an alien concept, than they do with full-service travel agencies that are ready (in theory, at least) to cater to your every whim.
- If you are a travel agent, buying for a client, you will naturally want to cut out as many middlemen as possible and deal with a wholesaler.
- If you are a member of the general public, you will find that wholesale consolidators and tour operators won't deal with you. You will either have to go through your travel agent or become a travel agent yourself. (See below and Chapter Nine.)

Why buy from consolidators?

In a word — savings! You will almost always get a better price from a consolidator than you will either from the airlines directly or from a travel agent who is using the airline-owned computer reservations system to conjure up a fare for you. The exception to the rule is when the airlines get into one of their periodic fare wars or an individual airline suddenly announces a special, usually time-limited, published fare. In these cases, consolidators (who often are locked in by contract in terms of what they can charge) can find themselves undersold.

If you don't at least investigate the consolidator market for every international flight you take, you are doing yourself a disservice. However, there are some circumstances in which consolidators make particularly good sense:

- *In the high season.* Then, ticket prices are normally inflated because of increased demand. If you are planning a family vacation abroad, consolidators will provide your best bet. Get some idea of what's available through the airlines, tour packages, etc. Then, shop aggressively for the best consolidator fare.

- *When you have to fly on short notice.* Unless you can get a last-minute courier bargain, consolidators are your best bet for savings. They can offer substantially lower prices than the airlines will charge you for a ticket purchased after the supersaver deadline. Be aware, however, of the differences between courier companies (discussed in the next chapter) and consolidators. As the flight date approaches, the courier company gets more and more nervous that it will have no one to fill that seat; consequently the fare goes down to lure someone into taking it. For a consolidator, on the other hand, a ticket becomes, if anything, more valuable as the flight date approaches. That's because the consolidator knows its best customers are those people who must purchase tickets at short notice. So don't expect the super deals you get from the courier companies. Expect instead to pay a fare somewhere close to the supersaver fare you might have gotten had you been able to book the flight earlier. Some consolidators specialize in selling seats only on flights that are leaving within the next 30 days.

- **When you're looking for an offbeat, bargain vacation.** There are some excellent deals to be had if you're willing to go off the beaten track — say to Turkey or Romania. The listings later in this chapter will point you to consolidators that specialize in specific regions of the world.

- **When you're looking at a long trip.** Long in terms of time, not distance. In these cases, you will most likely have to buy your outgoing and homebound tickets as separate one way tickets and here consolidators enjoy a clear advantage.

- **When you are planning to go around the world.** In this case, a consolidator that specializes in this type of journey may be your only option. Only a few airlines have routings that circle the globe but some consolidators make a specialty of stitching together one way fares from a number of airlines to create some very exciting 'round-the-world itineraries, which allow lengthy stopovers at intermediate points. If you are planning a trip to Australia, Southeast Asia, or India, you may be surprised how little more you will have to pay for a ticket that will take you on around the globe for your return trip.

- **When the whole family is traveling.** Even a small savings percentage-wise can be worth a few hundred dollars to you.

Tradeoffs

As with so much in this life, consolidator discounts aren't always a perfect solution for everybody in every circumstance. Here are some things that may (or may not) be negatives, depending on your needs and preferences.

- **Don't expect any great deals on First Class or Business**

Class. A few consolidators "specialize" in these seats, but the discounts are not the greatest. Feel lucky if you get as much as 10% off. Every once in a while, you may be able to save as much as 20%. By and large, though, the consolidator market is strictly coach.

- ***Many consolidators deal with foreign airlines.*** Some people just don't feel comfortable unless they are flying a major U.S., Canadian, or European airline. If you are one of these people, your choice of consolidator tickets will be somewhat more limited. You will also most likely pay a bit more. Many of the foreign carriers used by consolidators are every bit as professional, safety conscious, and reliable as their American counterparts. Others, notably those from some of the former Iron Curtain countries, have had their problems. Use your discretion and fly with airlines on which you feel safe. You will always know what airline you would be on before you buy the ticket.
- ***You're locked in to the airline on the ticket.*** Very few consolidator tickets allow you to change airlines.
- ***Refunds aren't always available.*** And, if they are, they are available only through the consolidator.
- ***You may have to pay by check, or even cash.*** This denies you the extra security that comes with using a credit card. A growing number of consolidators take plastic, but you may have to pay a slightly higher fare.
- ***True consolidators are small, independent operators, usually operating on wafer thin margins.*** Concepts like "total customer service" don't compute in these circumstances. So don't expect high levels of service. Also, some consolidators are recent immigrants who are better at shaving an extra dollar off a fare than they are at speaking English. What you interpret as rudeness may simply be a language barrier. All that being said, most consolidators (there are exceptions, of course) are honest. Once you get used to the peculiarities of this corner of the travel marketplace, you should have no problems.

Many airlines, especially the big ones, treat consolidator tickets (and the passengers holding them) differently from the way they do "regular" ones. Most of the limitations are minor and will not affect budget travelers who, after all, are more than willing to accept a few tradeoffs for a lower fare.

Here is a checklist of common restrictions that may — repeat, may — apply to some consolidator tickets. When planning your trip, determine if any of these things is important to you. If so, let the consolidator know. It may be able to accommodate you. Just be aware that you may be missing out on a lower fare to get the added "convenience."

- Do I need to get frequent flyer mileage credit for this trip?
- Do I want to have advance seating assignment?
- Do I need a direct flight (as opposed to making a connection)?
- Will I require a special meal during the flight?
- If there's a delay, will I need free meals or a room?
- Do I need a refundable ticket in case my plans change?

Frequent flyer mileage is an issue for some travelers. Of course, if you're flying on an obscure Eastern European or Middle Eastern airline, you probably wouldn't have much use for its frequent flyer miles anyway. Nonetheless, many consolidator tickets are sold on U.S. flag carriers or their so-called "travel partners" that offer frequent flyer miles. Why then can you get them with some consolidator tickets and not with others? The answer lies in the nature of the ticket you are buying. If you are purchasing a ticket that has been obtained at a "net fare" it may have attached to it a fare code that precludes frequent flyer miles. Remember that frequent flyer miles are, themselves, a form of discount or rebate. When the cost of a ticket drops below a certain point, the airline figures it doesn't pay to offer frequent flyer miles in addition to the low fare; the fare code attached to the ticket reflects that reasoning.

As noted earlier, however, some consolidator fares are actually the result of a rebate on the agent's commission. Some agencies, because of the large volume of business they bring to certain airlines, qualify for "overrides" or extra-large commissions. These commissions can go as high as 30% or 40%. In this case, the ticket is actually fairly high-priced. The savings you realize comes about because the agent doesn't take the entire commission to which she's entitled.

One way to tell which kind of ticket you have is to look at the fare box on the ticket itself. If it says "bulk" or "coach" or otherwise has no specific dollar amount, you probably have a consolidator ticket sold at a net fare. If there is a dollar figure on the ticket, higher than the price you paid, you have most likely received a rebate of the agent's override.

Some travelers are just as concerned about the comfort of the trip as they are with the price of the ticket. If you are among these folks, you will have to balance your savings against the length of the trip. Many consolidator tickets are cheaper in part because they involve flights that stop several times or require a change of planes and/or a roundabout routing. Sometimes you will have to choose between consolidator alternatives. For example, you might be able to fly from New York to Harare via London at a consolidator fare of $1200 or $1300 on a world-class airline. Or you could opt to fly on an Eastern European flag carrier, with a plane change in Sofia, for just $900. One fare is cheaper, but the flight is a good bit longer and involves a change of planes.

Finding consolidators

Consolidators are not really that hard to find. To help you get started, I have listed some contacts at the end of this chapter. But there are many more sources of cheap tickets than I have room for in this book. Many of them advertise in the travel section of your Sunday newspaper. New York and San Francisco are particularly active markets for consolidators, so you might want to go to your library and look up *The New York Times* and the *San Francisco Chronicle*. While you're at the library, get the phone books from some major cities and scan the travel agent listings for names like Mr. Cheaps and Cut-Throat Travel. That's a pretty good sign you've found a discount agency. London, too, is a great market for discount air fares — in fact, the whole bucket shop phenomenon began there. The London events magazine, *Time Out*, is packed with bucket shop ads and is available in many major cities here in the U.S.

The Association of Special Fares Agents (ASFA) maintains a web site at www.ntsltd.com/asfa/, where you can find consolidators not just in the United States and Canada but in places like Bhutan and Uzbekistan. Remember that the consolidator market is an international market. You can make arrangements with a London bucket shop by phone or fax and pick up your ticket when you get there. In fact, one reason some U.S. consolidators can offer such great prices is that they buy their tickets in foreign countries and have them shipped back.

Another great place to look for consolidators is in newspapers that cater to the ethnic group of the country to which you wish to travel. The national airlines in these countries will sometimes offer especially good deals to agencies operating in immigrant communities, knowing that the activity of these ethnic entrepreneurs is unlikely to cut into their "mainstream" market.

I have written an entire book devoted to consolidators, *Air Travel's Bargain Basement: The International Directory of Consolidators, Bucket Shops, and Other Sources of Discount Travel*. It lists well over 500 sources of cheap tickets in the U.S. and many more in Canada and around the world. The listings are cross-referenced by location and destinations served. There is also a separate listing of wholesale consolidators for those who can present themselves as travel agents (see below). For more information on this book, contact The Intrepid Traveler or log onto its main web site at www.intrepidtraveler.com.

Dealing with consolidators

The easiest way to deal with a consolidator is to use your favorite full-service travel agent instead! This assumes, of course, that you have established a good, on-going relationship with a knowledgeable travel agent who is committed to getting you the lowest possible fares in exchange for having your business year in, year out — including some business on which he or she can make a comfortable margin.

As noted earlier, many consolidators, including the country's largest, are strictly wholesale and will not deal directly with the public. So going through a travel agent automatically gives you access to a bigger market. And any travel agent can deal with any consolidator. If your travel agent refuses to get you a consolidator ticket, you obviously have not found the right travel agent yet.

Another reason to deal with a local travel agent is the sheer convenience. You make one call and you can often pick up the ticket (and pay for it) close to flight time. Also, a good travel agent will get to know your preferences and your needs. You will only have to outline the dos and don'ts one time. Your local travel agent may also be more knowledgeable than you about buying consolidator tickets and less likely to get you into a bad deal. This is not a universal rule, of course. Not all travel agents are equally knowledgeable.

Of course, you should expect to pay a little more through a full-service travel agent. That's only fair. Nonetheless, a consolidator ticket purchased through a travel agent should cost a good bit less than a "regular" ticket — otherwise what's the point?

That said, there's nothing keeping you from seeking out a "true" consolidator and getting as close to wholesale as possible. Besides, most consolidators are very much like your local travel agent anyway. That is, you can pick up the phone, tell them what you want, book a flight, pay for it with a credit card, and have it mailed to you. Location is not a problem (if time is not a factor) and most consolidators have toll-free 800 numbers. However, you may want to look for a consolidator close to you for the added convenience of local pickup.

Getting the best deal

Nothing beats concerted comparison shopping. But doing a little advance research can be invaluable. After all, you have no way of knowing how good the "discount" price is unless you know the "regular" price. Begin by calling a few airlines directly to inquire about fares. Then try some local full-service travel agencies, asking for the "best" fare they can give you. Skipping this step might cost you money.

Once you have an idea of the "fair market value" of the ticket you're looking for, use the listings in this book and start making calls. Get several quotes before deciding on the best deal. Don't allow yourself to be pressured into making a commitment before you're ready. After a few calls, you'll get the hang of it.

If you are a travel agent, you will naturally be looking for wholesalers. In theory, that's where you'll get the best deal. However, some consolidators sell to travel agents and the public at the same fares.

If you have a friend in the travel business, see if you get hold of the oddly named *Jax Fax* (see Chapter Ten). This monthly "travel marketing magazine" lists consolidator net fares being offered to the trade. They are conveniently broken down by destination. In fact, if you're an avid traveler, you might want to consider subscribing to *Jax Fax*. As I write this, *Jax Fax* is offering a two-year subscription for just $24. That's a small price to pay for a magazine that can save you hundreds if not thousands of dollars.

Jax Fax will let you know the "going rate," the net fares wholesale consolidators are offering to travel agents for destinations in which you are interested. As a consumer, you may not be able to get those fares, but they will serve as an indicator of how close you are getting to wholesale.

Now you are ready to start calling some consolidators. Just make sure you have organized all the information about dates and destinations and anything else you want the consolidator to know before you start making calls. If you are looking for the absolute cheapest fare, even if it means making connections, be sure to let the consolidator know. And don't forget about hotels at your destination. Many consolidators can get you discounts on your hotel stay. Some will sell you discounted hotel rooms even if you don't get your ticket from them! Ask.

Be a travel agent

If you were a travel agent, you'd be able to buy consolidator tickets at those mouth-watering net fares advertised in *Jax Fax*. The good news is that it is not too difficult to become a travel agent, at least on a part-time basis, without violating any rules of law or ethics. Once you have a business name and a business checking account you should have no problem buying tickets from wholesalers, even if they are for your own use. If this idea appeals to you, be sure to read Chapter Nine.

Risks and remedies

I am often asked, "Are consolidators reliable?" Well, sure, some consolidators go out of business. But then so do some airlines! The fact is, nothing's for certain. And I'm certainly not going to guarantee that nothing awful will happen to you if you use a consolidator. On the other hand, most have been around for a while and have sold thousands and thousands of tickets to people who had perfectly uneventful trips. So the odds are in your favor. Nonetheless, there are some precautions you can take if you're the nervous type:

- *Use a credit card to pay for your ticket.* Not all consolidators take credit cards. Of those that do, most will add a surcharge of 2% to 5% to cover the fee the credit card company charges them. The advantage of using a credit card is that you can stop payment if the ticket you receive is not the ticket you agreed on with the consolidator. The small extra cost may be worth the added security.

- *Find a consolidator close to home.* That way you can visit in person and reassure yourself that these are people you feel comfortable doing business with. Also, if something does go wrong, you'll have a desk to pound on.

- *Take out travel insurance.* Since consolidator tickets are invariably nonrefundable, if you get sick or have to cancel or change your plans for any reason, you can be out a bundle. Trip cancellation insurance can soften (if not eliminate) the blow. Just make sure you read the fine print and understand the restrictions.

- *Ask to get your tickets as soon as possible.* Again, the idea is that if something is wrong, you'll have time to get it fixed. If it's too close to flight time, you may face the choice of using the ticket as is or canceling the trip. Another way of saying the same thing is resist making full payment until you receive the tickets. If you are dealing with a local consolidator, don't turn over payment until you've had a chance to examine the tickets and make sure everything is as agreed.

- **Beware of altered tickets.** Examine handwritten tickets for any signs of erasures or changes. If it's a computer-generated ticket, look for stickers used to change the information in various fields. Erasures may render the ticket invalid and stickers are not allowed on tickets issued by American travel agencies. Talk to the consolidator, check with the airline, make sure you have a valid ticket.

- **Beware of coupon deals.** Sometimes the eye-popping fare being offered is tied to using a frequent flyer coupon that has been sold by its rightful owner. This is especially true of deep-discount offers in First Class and Business Class. The airlines say these coupons are non-transferable; others maintain that the free market is the free market. If you get caught, however, the airline can (and most often does) refuse to board you unless you pay the full unrestricted fare. So unless you are prepared to fight in court and pay full fare in the meantime, steer clear of these shady deals.

Consolidator listings

On the pages that follow I have listed a representative sampling of U.S. and Canadian sources of consolidator tickets. The term "consolidator" is used loosely here and the list contains many discount travel agencies as well as retail consolidators.

Due to space constraints, the list is far from comprehensive and the selection is, to some extent, arbitrary. Apologies to those consolidators not listed. A far more complete list, complete with helpful cross-referencing, will be found in my book, *Air Travel's Bargain Basement* (see above). The listing that follows is geographical by state and city, then alphabetical by company. The toll-free numbers provided may not work from all regions. The listing contains web sites, when known, and notes about destinations and specialties. I have tried to offer as broad a geographical selection as possible, listing U.S. consolidators first, then Canadian ones.

Note that the "Worldwide" designation in the listings does *not* include domestic tickets. Consolidators that sell domestic tickets are designated "US." So an entry may read "Worldwide, US." Destinations in parentheses are areas in which the consolidator is particularly strong. RTW means 'round the world.

Consolidators in the U.S.

Multiple Locations

	Austravel	800-633-3404 310-789-1710
	www.austravel.net	Australia, N. Zealand, S. Pacific
		10 locations
	Central Travel Network	877-735-9540
	www.4greatfares.com	C. & S. America (Mexico).
	www.vuelabarata.com	140 offices. Spanish spoken
	Council Travel	800-226-8624
	www.counciltravel.com	Worldwide student travel.
		60 locations
	PCS Travel	800-652-5725
		Asia, S. America, Europe, US
		10 locations
	STA Travel	800-781-4040
	www.statravel.com	Worldwide student travel.
		Locations in 18 states

Alabama

Huntsville	Blueskies Travel	800-538-7597 256-551-1775
	www.blueskies-travel.com	Worldwide

Arkansas

Little Rock	First Discount Travel	800-951-9558 501-219-1893
	www.1stdisctravel.com	Worldwide, US

Arizona

Phoenix	Panda Travel www.pandatravel.com	800-447-2632 Worldwide, US, cruises	602-943-3383
Tempe	Adventure Bound Tours www.adventure-bound.com	800-308-2345 Worldwide	480-968-3338

California

Albany	Avia Travel www.avia.com	800-950-2842 Asia, RTW, Africa	510-558-2150
Alhambra	APF Inc.	800-888-9168 Asia	626-282-9988
Beverly Hills	Air Travel Discounts www.airdisc.com	800-888-2621 Europe, Middle East, Asia, Africa	
Beverly Hills	Professional Travel Service www.pro-travel.com	800-289-0549 S. America	323-852-0549
Beverly Hills	Senator Travel www.senatortravel.com	800-736-2121 Europe, 1st & Business class	323-782-9500
Burbank	Cheap Tickets www.cheaptickets.com	800-377-1000 Worldwide, cruises	818-848-8080
Concord	Global Adventures Travel www.globaladv.com	800-989-6017 Worldwide, RTW, Circle Pacific	925-689-8883
Daly City	Custom Travel	Worldwide, charters, tours	415-239-4200
Fremont	King Tut Tours, Inc. www.kingtuttours.com	800-398-1888 Worldwide	510-791-2907
Fullerton	Cheap Tickets www.cheaptickets.com	800-377-1000 Worldwide	714-229-0131
Hollywood	Supersonic Travel	Worldwide, US, hotels	323-851-0333
Huntington Bch	Lotus International Tours www.lotustravel.com	800-450-4638 Middle East	714-892-8502
Irvine	Discover Wholesale Travel	800-576-7770 Asia, S. Pacific, S. America	949-833-1136
Los Angeles	Cheap Tickets www.cheaptickets.com	800-377-1000 Worldwide	310-645-5054
Los Angeles	Japan Express	Asia (Japan), S. America	213-680-0550

California (cont'd)

Los Angeles	Jetway Tours	800-421-8771	818-990-2918
		Europe, S. America, S.E. Asia	
Los Angeles	Levon Travel	800-445-3866	323-871-8711
	www.levontravel.com	Europe, Middle East, Armenia, US	
Los Angeles	New Frontiers USA	800-677-0720	310-670-7318
	www.newfrontiers.com	Europe (England, France, Italy)	
Los Angeles	Tokyo Travel Service	800-227-2065	213-680-3545
		Asia	
Los Angeles	Tradesco Tours	800-833-3402	310-649-5808
	www.tradescotours.com	Eastern Europe	
Los Angeles	Travel Associates	800-992-7388	323-933-7388
	www.travelassociates.com	US, Hawaii, Caribbean	
Northridge	Cheap Seats	800-451-7200	818-717-8591
	www.cheapseatstravel.com	US	
Palo Alto	Scan The World	800-775-0200	650-325-0876
	www.scantheworld.com	Europe, Africa, Australia, RTW, US	
Pasadena	Holiday Tours	800-393-1212	626-795-1012
		C. & S. America	
San Anselmo	The Budget Traveler		415-331-3700
		Europe, C. America	
San Bruno	Cheap Tickets	800-377-1000	650-588-3700
	www.cheaptickets.com	Worldwide, cruises	
San Diego	Fare Deal Travel	800-243-2785	619-282-8866
	www.faredealtravel.com	Europe, Caribbean, US	
San Diego	Travel Network	800-338-7987	619-299-5161
		Asia	
San Francisco	Air Brokers International	800-883-3273	415-397-1383
	www.airbrokers.com	RTW, Asia,Australia, S. America	
San Francisco	Airbound		415-834-9445
	www.airbound.com	Worldwide, US	
San Francisco	Alta Tours	800-338-4191	415-777-1307
	www.altatours.com	S. America (Argentina, Chile)	
San Francisco	Cheap Tickets	800-377-1000	415-896-5023
	www.cheaptickets.com	Worldwide, cruises	
San Francisco	China Travel Service	800-899-8618	415-352-8618
	www.chinatravelservice.com	Asia, hotels, charters	

California (cont'd)

San Francisco	Cut-Throat Travel	800-642-8747	415-989-8747
	Worldwide, India		
San Francisco	Festival of Asia	800-533-9953	415-908-6980
	www.asiafest.com	Asia, Australia, S. Pacific, India	
San Francisco	High Adventure	800-350-0612	415-912-5600
	www.highadv.com	RTW, adventure travel	
San Francisco	Skytours Travel	800-246-8687	415-454-4932
	www.skytours.com	Europe, S. America, Asia	
San Francisco	South Pacific Express Tvl	800-321-7739	415-982-6833
	www.1stoptravel.com	S. Pacific, Europe, US	
San Francisco	Sun Destination Travel		415-398-1313
	www.sundestination.com	Worldwide, US	
San Francisco	Ticket Planet	800-799-8888	415-288-9999
	www.ticketplanet.com	Worldwide, RTW, Circle Pacific	
San Francisco	Vacationland	800-245-0050	415-788-0503
	www.vacation-land.com	Asia, S.E. Asia, Europe (London)	
San Jose	Suntrips	800-786-8747	408-432-1101
	www.suntrips.com	Hawaii, C. America (Mex), Europe	
Santa Ana	Aloha Continental Travel	800-287-0275	714-565-3737
	www.alohacontinental.com	Europe, US	
Santa Clarita	Discount Travel	800-227-3235	310-641-5343
	www.rebeltours.com	Europe, charters	
Santa Monica	Continental Travel Shop		310-453-8655
	Europe		
Santa Monica	Flight Coordinators	800-544-3644	310-581-5600
	www.flightcoordinators.com	Worldwide	
Sherman Oaks	Brazil Tours	800-927-8352	818-990-4995
	www.braziltours.com	S. America	
S. San Fran.	Natrabu Indonesian	800-628-7228	650-872-7790
	S.E. Asia		
Valencia	Rebel Tours & Travel	800-227-3235	661-294-0900
	www.rebeltours.com	Europe (Holland)	

Colorado

Aurora	Overseas Travel	800-783-7196	303-337-7196
	Europe, Africa, Asia, S. America		

Colorado (cont'd)

Denver	Affinity Travel www.irantravel.com	303-639-1000 Middle East (Iran, the Gulf)	
Denver	Mile High Tours	800-777-8687 303-758-8246 US, Las Vegas, C. America (Mex)	
Denver	Mr. Cheap's Travel www.mrcheaps.com	800-672-4327 303-758-3833 US, Worldwide, last minute	
Englewood	Fare Deals Travel www.faredealstravel.com	800-878-2929 303-792-2929 Worldwide, US	

Connecticut

New Milford	The Africa Desk www.africadesk.com	800-284-8796 860-354-9341 Africa	
Ridgefield	All Destinations www.alldestinations.com	800-228-1510 203-431-2401 Caribbean, US, C. & S. America	
Wash. Depot	Tread Lightly Ltd. www.treadlightly.com	800-643-0060 860-868-1710 C. & S. America, Asia (Mongolia)	
Westport	Inclusive Holidays	800-238-2140 203-454-2233 Caribbean, Europe	
Wilton	International Ventures	800-727-5475 203-761-1110 S. Africa, Kenya (Nairobi)	

District of Columbia

Washington	Americas Travel Services	800-704-6484 202-955-3815 C. & S. America	
Washington	Bethany Travel Agency	202-223-3336 Worldwide	
Washington	Democracy Travel	800-536-8728 202-965-7200 RTW, Circle Pacific, Worldwide	
Washington	Fana Travels www.fanatravels.com	800-600-3262 202-667-0101 Europe, Africa, Middle East, India	
Washington	Ghana America Vacations	888-774-4262 202-862-4959 Africa	
Washington	PERS Travel Inc.	800-583-0909 202-338-2121 Middle East (Iran)	
Washington	Value Travel www.airfaresbrazil.com	800-887-5686 202-887-0065 C. & S. America (Brazil)	

District of Columbia (cont'd)

Washington	Worldwide Travel, Inc.	800-343-0038	202-659-6430
		Worldwide, US	

Florida

Boynton Bch.	Palm Coast Travel	800-444-1560	561-733-9950
		Europe (Scan.), Asia, S. America	
Coral Gables	Interworld Travel www.interworldtravel.com	800-468-3796	305-443-4929
		Europe (UK). Africa, C.&S. America	
Coral Gables	Karell Travel www.karell.com	800-327-0373	305-446-7766
		S. Africa	
Ft. Lauderdale	Brazilian Wave Tours & Tvl	800-682-3315	954-561-3788
		S. America (Brazil)	
Ft. Lauderdale	Hostway Travel www.hostwaytravel.com	800-327-3207	954-966-8500
		Worldwide, US, cruises	
Ft. Lauderdale	North Star Tours www.passagetours.com	800-431-1511	954-351-7131
		Europe (Scandinavia)	
Ft. Walton Bch	RTS Travel Services www.yourvacation.com	800-853-1128	850-729-8722
		Worldwide, US	
Lake Worth	Intourist USA www.intourist-usa.ru	800-556-5305	561-585-5305
		Europe (Russia), Asia (China)	
Longwood	Travel World www.travelworlds.com	800-628-3002	407-628-2431
		Africa, Middle East, India, Asia	
Miami	2000 Latin Tours	800-254-7378	305-670-4488
		Worldwide, C. & S. America, Carib.	
Miami	Travel People www.travelpeople1.com	800-999-9912	305-596-4800
		Europe.Africa, Asia, S. America	
Miami Beach	Mirabel Travel	800-890-4590	305-937-4880
		Europe, Middle East (Israel)	
Naples	Europe On Line	800-587-4849	941-263-3937
		Europe fr. Florida, LA, Anchorage	
Orlando	Travac Tours & Charters www.thetravelsite.com	800-872-8800	407-896-0014
		Worldwide	
Tampa	Number One Travel www.onetravelworld.com	800-475-1009	813-872-6900
		Asia, China, Korea	
Tampa	Passport Travel Mgmt	800-950-5864	813-931-3166
		Asia, S. Pacific	

Florida (cont'd)

Vero Beach	Air Travel Discounts www.airdisc.com	800-888-2621 Europe, Middle East, Asia, Africa	561-794-9345

Georgia

Atlanta	EconomyTravel.com www.economytravel.com	888-222-2110 Worldwide	770-290-7730
Atlanta	Hari World Travel www.hariworld.com	India, Europe	404-233-5005
Atlanta	Japan Travel Service	800-822-3336 Japan, Asia	770-451-3607
Atlanta	Midtown Tvl Consultants	800-548-8904 Worldwide	404-872-8308
Atlanta	Regent Travel Network www.regenttours.com	Asia	404-248-8062
Atlanta	Skyway Travel	Asia, Europe, Middle East, Africa	404-252-2152
Atlanta	South American Fiesta	800-334-3782 C. & S. America, hotels	770-321-6814
Atlanta	TMV Tours www.tmvtours.com	Middle East, Asia, Africa, India	404-256-4809
Atlanta	World Connections	800-777-8892 Asia, US	770-393-8892
Marietta	Alpha Travel www.alpha4travel.com	800-793-8424 US, Europe, Africa, Mid East, India	770-988-9982

Hawaii

Honolulu	Cheap Tickets www.cheaptickets.com	800-377-1000 Worldwide, cruise dept.	808-947-3717
Honolulu	Pali Tours & Travel	Worldwide	808-533-3608
Honolulu	Riverside Travel	Worldwide, US	808-521-5645
Kahului, Maui	Cheap Tickets www.cheaptickets.com	800-377-1000 Worldwide, cruises	808-242-8094

Iowa

| Cedar Rapids | Globe Travels | | 319-362-9071 |
| | www.globetravels.com | Europe, Asia, India, US | |

Illinois

Buffalo Grove	Hana Travel	800-962-8044	847-913-1177
		Asia, hotels	
Carbondale	Borgsmiller Travels	800-228-0585	618-529-5511
	www.mta-tvl.com	Asia (Malaysia)	
Carbondale	Malaysia Travel Advisors	888-359-8655	618-351-9398
	www.emalaysiatravel.com	S.E. Asia (Malaysia)	
Chicago	Chisholm Travel	800-631-2824	312-321-1800
	www.chisholmair.net	Asia, S. Pacific, Pacific Rim	
Chicago	Egypt Tours & Travel	800-523-4978	773-506-9999
	www.egypttours.com	Middle East (Egypt, Israel)	
Chicago	Jaya Travel	877-359-5292	
	www.jayatravel.com	Worldwide, US	
Chicago	Mena Tours & Travel	800-937-6362	773-275-2125
	www.menatours.net	C. & S. America	
Chicago	National Travel Centre	800-228-6886	312-939-2190
		Asia, S. Pacific	
Chicago	Overseas Express	800-343-4873	773-262-4971
	www.ovex.com	Europe, Africa, Middle East, Asia	
Chicago	Safariline	877-723-2745	
	www.safarilinetravel.com	Africa, Mediterr., Spain, Turkey	
Chicago	TMV Tours		773-785-6400
	www.tmvtours.com	Middle East, Asia, Africa, India	
Chicago	Trade Wind Associates	800-438-4853	312-819-9588
	www.twai.com	Worldwide, US	
Chicago	Travel Avenue	800-333-3335	312-876-6866
	www.travelavenue.com	Worldwide, US	
Chicago	Travel Center, Inc.	800-621-5228	312-726-0088
		Worldwide, Asia, India	
Deerfield	Cut Rate Travel	800-388-0575	847-405-0575
		Worldwide (exc Can., Mex., Carib.)	
Lincolnshire	Travel Core of America	888-700-8747	
		S. Africa, Europe	

Illinois (cont'd)

Lyons	Unlimited World Travel	800-322-3557	708-442-7715
		Worldwide, US	
Rosemont	DER Travel Services	800-717-4247	847-430-0000
	www.dertravel.com	Worldwide	
Rosemont	Online Travel	800-660-5300	847-318-8890
	www.eurorail.com	Europe, Middle East, C. & S. Am	

Indiana

Mishawaka	U.S. Int'l Travel	800-759-7373	219-255-7272
	www.travelconsolidators.com	Europe, Middle East	

Kansas

Overland Park	Dollar Saver Travel		913-381-5050
	www.dstravel.com	India	
Overland Park	Winggate Travel		913-451-9200
	www.winggatetravel.com	Asia, Europe	

Louisiana

Baton Rouge	Discount Travel	888-738-8747	522-761-4711
		US, Las Vegas; cruises, tours	
New Orleans	Uniglobe Americana		504-561-8100
		Worldwide	

Massachusetts

Boston	Kutrubes Travel	800-878-8566	617-426-5668
	www.kutrubestravel.com	Europe (Greece), Mid East (Leb.)	
Boston	Spector Travel	800-879-2374	617-338-0111
	www.spectortravel.com	Africa	
Boston	TMV Tours		617-426-6181
	www.tmvtours.com	Middle East, Asia, Africa, India	

Maryland

Baltimore	AESU Travel	800-638-7640	410-366-5494
	www.aesu.com	Europe, student groups	
Bethesda	Dan Travel	800-362-1308	301-907-8977
	www.dantravel.com	C. & S. America	

Maryland (cont'd)

Hanover	Student Travel Services www.stsvacations.com	800-648-4849 Caribbean	410-859-4200
Landover	Kambi Travel International	800-220-2192 Europe, Asia, Africa (W. Africa)	301-925-9012
Landover	Sharp Travel	877-356-2165 Worldwide, US	301-731-3355
Owings Mills	Fare Deals Ltd. www.faredeal.com	800-347-7006 Caribbean, US, Hawaii, Worldwide	410-581-8787
Rockville	Hans World Travel www.hanstravel.com	800-421-4267 Europe, Asia	301-770-1717
Rockville	Monica Travel & Tours	Worldwide, US	301-294-1166
Rockville	Triple C Travel www.travelctravel.com	800-638-9580 Asia, US	301-279-7652
Silver Spring	Sona Travels www.hanstravel.com	800-720-7662 Europe, MEast, S. Amer., India, US	301-589-3344

Michigan

Holland	GTI Travel Consolidators	800-829-8234 Europe, Eastern Europe, Asia	616-396-1492
Southfield	Jaya Travel www.jayatravel.com	877-359-5292 Worldwide, US	
Troy	Travel Charter International www.travelcharter.com	800-521-5267 Charters to Eur, Carib, C. America	248-641-9600

Minnesota

Bloomington	Kristensen Int'l Tvl & Tours www.kitt-travel.com	800-262-8728 S. Pacific, Australia, N. Zealand	612-854-5589
Minneapolis	Campus Travel	800-328-3359 Europe fr. Minneapolis	612-338-5616
Minnetonka	Travel Fore Seasons	800-328-1332 Eastern Europe, CIS	651-439-4634
Wayzata	Travel Beyond	800-823-6063 Africa (S. Africa), S. America	952-475-9975

Missouri

Oak Grove	Group & Leisure Travel	800-874-6608 Worldwide, US	816-690-4040
St. Louis	Unitravel www.unitravel.com	800-325-2222 Worldwide, US	314-569-2501

Montana

Kalispell	Integrity Travel www.integ-travel.com	800-468-4272 Worldwide	406-755-8484

Nevada

Las Vegas	Lowestfare.com www.lowestfare.com	800-569-3783 US, Worldwide	
Reno	Mr. Cheap's Travel	800-672-4327 US, Europe	503-557-9101

New Jersey

Cherry Hill	SAF Travel World	800-394-8587 Asia (Philippines, Viet), Europe, US	609-216-2900
Edison	Rupa Travel Service www.rupatravels.com	Worldwide, US	732-572-5000
Edison	TMV Tours www.tmvtours.com	Middle East, Asia, Africa, India	908-603-8484
Hackensack	Sunny Land Tours www.sunnylandtours.com	800-783-7839 Worldwide, adventure travel	201-487-2150
Jersey City	Aviation Travels & Tours	Worldwide	201-418-8167
Jersey City	Garden State Travel www.gardenstatetravel.com	Asia	201-333-1232
Jersey City	Marakesh Tourist Company www.marakeshtouristco.com	800-458-1772 Europe, Middle East	201-435-2800
Jersey City	TMV Tours www.tmvtours.com	Middle East, Asia, Africa, India	201-222-2550
N. Bergen	Gama Tours www.israelplus.com	800-747-7235 Israel	201-662-1000
Parsippany	Paul Laifer Tours www.laifertours.com	800-346-6314 Europe (Eastern), hotels	973-887-1188

New Jersey (cont'd)

Rahway	Rahway Travel www.rahwaytravel.com	800-526-2786 Europe (Eastern & Ukraine)	732-381-8800
Ramsey	Prime Travel www.primetravel.com	800-344-3962 Europe, Middle East, Asia, CIS	201-825-1600
West Orange	Worldvision Travel Services www.airfareworldvision.com	800-545-7118 Europe, Africa, Asia, US	973-736-8210

New York

Astoria	Crown Peters Travel	800-321-1199 Europe, Middle East, Cairo, Istanbul	718-932-7800
Astoria	P&F International	800-444-6666 Europe, Middle East, C. & S. Amer	718-937-1998
Beacon	Oxford Travel www.oxfordtvl.com	800-851-5290 Europe, Africa, S. America, Asia	914-838-1122
Beacon	Travel 'N Tours	800-984-9075 Europe, Asia, Africa, S. America	914-838-2600
Brooklyn	Falcon Travel & Tours	Worldwide	718-522-0692
Cedarhurst	Perfect Travel www.1800elalfly.com	800-352-5359 Middle East (Israel)	212-840-6777
Douglaston	Vytis Tours www.vytistours.com	800-778-9847 Europe (Scan, Baltics, Russia)	718-423-6161
Forest Hills	Spanish Heritage Tours www.shtours.com	800-221-2580 Europe (Spain & Portugal)	718-544-2752
Fresh Mdws	The Egyptian Connection www.egyptontheweb.com	800-334-4477 Worldwide, US	718-762-3848
Lewiston	Raptim Travel	800-777-9232 Worldwide (religious travel)	716-754-9232
New City	Pinto Basto USA www.pousada.com	800-526-8539 Europe, C. America	914-639-8020
New York	Air Travel Discounts www.airdisc.com	800-888-2621 Europe, Middle East, Asia, Africa	212-922-1326
New York	Air-Supply www.air-supply.com	Europe, Africa, S.E. Asia, Australia	212-695-1647
New York	Airfares Inc. www.tourdeal.com	800-753-0578 Europe (Central)	212-213-3865

New York (cont'd)

New York	Am-Jet Travels	800-414-4147	212-697-5332
	Middle East, India, Asia, US		
New York	Amba Travel		212-868-2500
	Europe, Asia (India)		
New York	Arrow Travel		212-889-2550
	Worldwide, US		
New York	ATC Travel	800-826-6388	212-967-1200
	C. & S. America, Europe		
New York	Azure Travel Bureau	800-882-1427	212-239-1999
	www.azuretravel.com	India, Nepal, Tibet	
New York	B & D Tours	800-548-6877	212-953-3300
	Worldwide, 1st & Business		
New York	Balkan USA	800-822-1106	212-586-3522
	www.balkanusa.com	Europe (Bulgaria & Romania)	
New York	Carbone Travel	800-735-8899	212-213-4310
	www.carbone-travel.com	S. America	
New York	Central Europe Holidays	800-800-8891	212-725-0948
	www.tourdeal.com	Europe (Eastern), spa tours	
New York	Cheap Tickets	800-377-1000	212-570-1179
	www.cheaptickets.com	Worldwide	
New York	Cloud Tours Travel	800-223-7880	212-753-6104
	www.cloudtours.com	Mediterranean, MIddle East	
New York	Club America Travel	800-221-4969	212-972-2865
	www.clubamericatravel.com	Middle East (Turkey)	
New York	CWT Vacations	800-223-6862	212-695-8435
	Worldwide, US		
New York	Discount Tickets	888-382-4327	212-391-2313
	www.discounttickets1.com	US, last minute	
New York	Downtown Travel	800-952-3519	212-766-5705
	Europe, Asia (Aeroflot, Finnair)		
New York	Earth Travel	800-203-1518	212-594-3553
	Asia		
New York	Ferndale Travel	800-790-1016	360-384-0414
	Europe (Scandinavia), S. America		
New York	Fly Wise Travel	800-347-3939	212-869-2223
	www.checkairfare.com	US, Worldwide, last minute	

New York (cont'd)

New York	Flytime Tour & Travel	800-786-4388	212-760-3737
	Europe, Asia		

New York	Glavs Travel	800-336-5727	212-290-3300
	www.glavs.com	Europe, Asia (Russia & CIS)	

New York	Hari World Travel		212-957-3000
	www.hariworld.com	India, Europe	

New York	Himalayan Intl Tours		212-564-5164
	www.himalayantours.com	Asia, India	

New York	Homeric Tours & Charters	800-223-5570	212-753-1100
	www.homerictours.com	Europe (Greece), Middle East	

New York	Inka's Empire Tours		646-638-0035
	www.inkas.com	S. America (Peru, Bolivia)	

New York	Intl Tvl Exchange	800-727-7830	212-808-5368
	www.flyite.com	US, Europe, Africa, Middle East	

New York	Jaya Travel	800-359-5292	
	www.jayatravel.com	Worldwide, US	

New York	L. T. & Travel	800-295-3436	212-682-2748
	www.airfaredomestic.com	Caribbean, US, Hawaii	

New York	Magical Holidays	800-228-2208	212-486-9600
	Africa, Europe		

New York	Mercury Tours & Travel	877-711-8687	212-268-7434
	US		

New York	Moment's Notice		212-486-0500
	www.moments-notice.com	Worldwide, Hawaii, Caribbean, US	

New York	New Europe Holidays	800-642-3874	212-686-2424
	Europe, Middle East, Asia		

New York	New Frontiers USA	800-366-6387	212-779-0600
	www.newfrontiers.com	Europe (UK, France, Italy)	

New York	Now Voyager		212-431-1616
	www.nowvoyagertravel.com	US, Worldwide	

New York	O'Connor Fairways Travel	800-662-0550	212-661-0550
	www.oconnors.com	Europe (Ireland, UK)	

New York	Orbis Polish Travel Bureau	800-867-6526	212-867-5011
	www.orbis-usa.com	Europe (Poland, Eastern), hotels	

New York	Pacific Holidays	800-355-8025	212-764-1977
	www.pacificholidaysinc.com	Asia, mainly packages	

NewYork (cont'd)

New York	Panorama Travel www.panoramatravel.com	800-204-7130 Europe (E. & Russia), Asia (Central)	212-741-0033
New York	Peru Unlimited	800-947-5655 S. America	212-995-9786
New York	Pino Welcome Travel www.pinotravel.com	800-247-6578 Europe (Italy), S. Am, Asia, Africa	212-682-5400
New York	Prestige Tour & Travel www.prestigetour.com	800-232-9638 Africa	212-779-8371
New York	Sharp Travel Headquarters www.sharp-travel.com	800-736-1343 S.E. Asia	212-465-9500
New York	Super Travel & Tours	800-878-7371 Pakistan, Africa	212-986-8002
New York	The French Experience www.frenchexperience.com	800-283-7262 France	212-986-3800
New York	Tourlite International www.tourlite.com	800-272-7600 Mediterranean, S. & C. America	212-599-2727
New York	Trade Wind Associates www.twai.com	800-438-4853 Worldwide, US	212-286-0667
New York	Travac Tours & Charters www.thetravelsite.com	800-872-8800 Europe, S. & C. America	212-563-3303
New York	Travel Abroad	800-297-8788 Europe, India, US	212-564-8989
New York	Tulips Travel www.tulipstravel.com	800-882-3383 S.E. Asia, Worldwide, US	212-490-3388
New York	United Tours Corp.	Europe (Eastern, Russia)	212-245-1100
New York	WalkerHill Worldwide Tvl www.wwtny.com	800-568-2835 Asia, Worldwide, US	212-221-1234
New York	World Trade Tours	800-732-7386 C. & S. America	212-889-8025
New York	Zohny Travel	800-963-6348 Middle East, Africa, Asia, India, US	212-953-0077
Oceanside	Detours	800-252-8780 Worldwide	516-763-1900
Rego Park	Zig Zag Travel	800-726-0249 Worldwide, US	718-575-3434

New York (cont'd)

White Plains	Abratours	800-227-2887	914-949-3300
		Middle East, Europe (Greece)	

White Plains	EuroGroups	800-462-2577	914-682-7456
	www.eurogroups.com	Europe, groups of 10+ only	

Yonkers	Benyo World Travel	800-872-8925	914-968-0175
	www.benyo.com	Europe (Eastern)	

Ohio

Beachwood	Discover Africa	888-330-4880	216-595-9775
	www.discafrica.com	Africa	

Beachwood	Travel Planner	800-336-2757	216-831-9336
		Europe, Middle East (Israel)	

Cleveland	American Travel	877-781-7181	216-781-7181
		Europe, Asia	

Cleveland	Safariline	877-723-2745	
	www.safarilinetravel.com	Africa, Mediterranean	

Cleveland	Traveline Travel	877-723-2745	440-461-8811
	www.travelinetravel.com	S. Africa, Europe, C. & S. America	

Lakewood	Adventure Intl Tvl Service	800-542-2487	216-228-7171
		Europe (Eastern)	

Lakewood	Panorama World Trs & Tvl	800-475-9339	216-228-9339
	www.panoramaholidays.com	Europe, Asia, ME, S. Pacific, Africa	

Woodmere	Elite Tours & Travel	800-354-8320	216-514-9000
		Middle East	

Oregon

Aloha	First Discount Travel	888-819-4646	503-848-4646
	www.1discount-travel.com	Worldwide, US	

Portland	Nova Travel	800-334-1188	503-697-4460
	www.novatravel.com	Asia, India	

Portland	Unique Travel	800-397-1719	503-221-1719
		Asia, China, Russia	

Pennsylvania

Ardmore	DownUnder Direct	800-642-6224	610-896-1741
	www.swainaustralia.com	Australia, S. Pacific	

Pennsylvania (cont'd)

Ardmore	Swain Australia Tours www.swainaustralia.com	800-227-9246	610-896-9595
	Australia, New Zealand, S. Pacific		
N. Huntingdon	Holiday Travel Intl www.holidaytvl.com	800-775-7111	724-863-7500
	US, Las Vegas, Reno		
Paoli	Pennsylvania Travel www.patravel.com	800-331-0947	610-251-9944
	Worldwide		
Philadelphia	Premier Travel Services www.premiertours.com	800-545-1910	215-893-9966
	Southern Africa		
Philadelphia	SAF Travel World		215-440-7600
	Asia (Philippines, Vietnam)		
Plymouth Mtg	1-800-Airfare www.800airfare.com	800-247-3273	610-270-8700
	Europe, Asia, S. America, US/ Can		

Tennessee

Chattanooga	Travel Network	423-485-1291
	www.airlineconsolidator.com Worldwide	

Texas

Brentwood	Air Discounters International		915-643-1007
	www.airdiscounters.com	Worldwide (exc Carib & Hawaii)	
College Station	ITS Tours & Travel	800-533-8688	979-764-0518
	Europe (Russia), Asia (CIS), India		
Dallas	D-FW Tours www.dfwtours.com	800-527-2589	972-980-4540
	Worldwide (exc. Hawaii)		
Dallas	Royal Lane Travel	800-329-2030	214-340-2030
	Worldwide		
Dallas	TCI Travel	800-333-7033	214-630-3344
	Europe, Middle East, Africa		
Houston	EST International Travel		713-974-0521
	Worldwide, charters, packages		
Houston	Frosch International Travel www.froschtravel.com	800-866-1623	713-850-1566
	S. Africa, Middle East (Israel), hotels		
Houston	Katy Van Tours	800-808-8747	281-492-7032
	Europe, Asia, Middle East		
Houston	Latin American Travel	800-252-0775	713-774-0600
	C. & S. America, Caribbean		

Texas (cont'd)

Houston	Trade Wind Associates www.twai.com	800-438-4853 Worldwide, US	713-960-0343
Irving	Overseas Express www.ovex.com	800-750-1224 Europe, Africa, Middle East, Asia	972-819-2000
Plano	Embassy Tours www.embassytravel.com	800-299-5284 C. & S. America	972-985-2929
Trophy Club	Carefree Getaway Travel www.carefree.com	800-969-8687 Europe, Asia, US	817-430-5828

Utah

Salt Lake City	Jensen Baron Travel Exp	800-333-2060 Worldwide	801-267-5757

Virginia

Alexandria	International Discount Tvl	800-466-7357 Europe, S. America	703-750-0101
Annandale	Asia Specialists	800-969-7427 Asia	703-941-2323
Annandale	Sharp Travel Agency	800-969-7427 Asia, India, US	703-941-2323
Arlington	Gerosa Tours	800-243-7672 S. America, Europe	703-415-4795
Baileys Xrds	Wholesale Travel Centre www.airfare.com	800-886-4988 Europe, Africa, Middle East, Asia	703-379-6363
Burke	Transview Travel	888-359-2759 Worldwide, Pakistan, India	703-912-3900
Fredericksburg	Travel Network www.travnet.com	800-929-1290 Worldwide (exc MidEast & Africa)	540-891-2929
Richmond	Fellowship Travel Intl www.fellowship.com	800-446-7667 Worldwide, missionary travel	804-264-0121

Washington

Bellevue	Travel Network www.travel-network.com	800-933-5963 US, Caribbean, C. & S. America	425-643-1600
Seattle	Americas Tours & Travel www.latinfares.com	800-553-2513 C. & S. America, hotels, tours	206-623-8850

Washington (cont'd)

Seattle	Around the World Travel www.justfares.com	800-766-3601	206-223-3600 RTW, Europe, Asia , India, Africa
Seattle	Cheap Tickets www.cheaptickets.com	800-377-1000	206-467-7979 Worldwide, cruises
Seattle	EZ Travel www.ezvoyage.com		206-524-1977 Middle East, Worldwide, US
Seattle	New Wave Travel	800-220-9283	206-527-3579 Worldwide, Asia
Seattle	Red Star Travel	800-215-4378 Europe (CIS), Asia (CIS), China	
Seattle	Travel Team www.travelteam.com	800-788-0829	206-301-0443 Worldwide, US

Wisconsin

Mequon	Value Holidays www.valhol.com	800-558-6850	262-241-6373 Europe (Western), Worldwide
Milwaukee	Pleasure Break Vacations www.pleasurebreak.com	800-777-1566	414-934-1882 Europe, Africa, ME, C. America

Consolidators in Canada

Alberta

Calgary	Travel CUTS www.travelcuts.com	800-667-2887	403-531-2070 Worldwide student travel
Edmonton	Butte Travel Service www.buttetravel.ab.ca	800-661-8906	780-477-3561 Worldwide, Europe (serves Western Canada)
Edmonton	Travel CUTS www.travelcuts.com	800-667-2887	780-439-3096 Worldwide student travel

British Columbia

Richmond	Cannetic Travel	888-279-9902	604-279-0066 Asia (China, Hong Kong)
Vancouver	Pacesetter Travel www.goaway.com	800-663-5115	604-687-3083 S. Pacific, Africa, Asia

British Columbia(cont'd)

Vancouver	Trade Wind Associates www.twai-canada.com	800-268-4853 Worldwide	604-683-6900
Vancouver	Travel CUTS www.travelcuts.com	800-667-2887 Worldwide student travel	604-659-2887
Victoria	Blaney's Travel Plus blaneystravel.com	800-376-6177 Worldwide	250-382-7254

Manitoba

Winnipeg	Travel CUTS www.travelcuts.com	800-667-2887 Worldwide student travel	204-783-5353

Nova Scotia

Halifax	Travel CUTS www.travelcuts.com	800-667-2887 Worldwide student travel	902-494-2054

Ontario

Kingston	Odyssey Travel www.odyssey-travel.com	Worldwide, RTW	613-549-3553
North York	The Last Minute Club www.lastminuteclub.com	800-563-2582 Worldwide (members only)	416-441-2582
Ottawa	Odyssey Travel www.odyssey-travel.com	Worldwide, RTW	613-789-1900
Ottawa	Travel CUTS www.travelcuts.com	800-667-2887 Worldwide student travel	613-238-8222
Toronto	Trade Wind Associates www.twai-canada.com	800-268-4853 Worldwide, Canada/US	416-966-4853
Toronto	Travel CUTS www.travelcuts.com	800-667-2887 Worldwide student travel	416-979-2406

Quebec

Montreal	Chad & Calden www.chad-calden.com	(no phone, Internet only) Worldwide	
Montreal	Travel CUTS www.travelcuts.com	800-667-2887 Worldwide student travel	514-284-1368
Quebec City	Travel CUTS www.travelcuts.com	800-667-2887 Worldwide student travel	418-654-0224

Chapter Seven

Air Couriers

How would you like to be able to fly from New York to Chile for just $100 roundtrip? Or from San Francisco to Bangkok for $148?

Well, it's possible. I know because I've done it. It's even possible (although increasingly rare) to fly for free. How? By traveling as an air courier.

Even though the "golden age" of air courier travel is past and real bargains increasingly hard to come by, the flexible flyer can still nab some great fares.

What is an air courier?

An air courier is a member of the general public who accompanies time-sensitive business cargo being shipped by reputable freight companies as passengers' baggage aboard regularly scheduled commercial airlines to international destinations. Although little known to most travelers, air courier shipments have been going on for decades. They are a well-established and perfectly respectable niche in the air freight business.

Why not just use FedEx? you may ask. Obviously, a lot of people do. But there are customers who prefer to deal with smaller boutique shipping operations that can afford them a greater level of personal attention than can a massive operation like Fed Ex, DHL, or the other mega-shippers.

These smaller shippers, the air courier companies of which we speak, like to use regularly scheduled commercial airliners for a number of reasons. Most obvious is that the air courier companies do not have their own fleet of planes. Cargo airlines (there are quite a few) offer haphazard schedules, cumbersome paperwork and procedures, and often can't guarantee expedited handling. The passenger carrying airlines, in contrast, fly on a regular or even daily basis to major destinations and have plenty of space in their holds for cargo.

Since air courier companies are, by definition, in the business of *expedited* shipping, they do not send their shipments as regular cargo. Instead, they send it as passengers' baggage. On a commercial airliner, passengers' baggage enjoys several advantages over regular cargo. It can be loaded on board at literally the last minute before flight time. At the destination, passengers' baggage comes off the plane first and goes immediately to customs for clearance. For the air courier company, these advantages can mean the difference between being able to promise their customers next-day delivery, as opposed to day-and-a-half or two-day delivery. What's more, shipping cargo as passengers' baggage creates a "paper trail" that offers the air courier company and its customers greater assurance that the package will get where it's supposed to go when it's supposed to get there.

It's a great system, but there's a problem. The bureaucratic mind being what it is, neither the airlines nor customs agencies around the world will treat a piece of cargo as passengers' baggage unless they see a living, breathing passenger traveling with it.

That's where you come in. Rather than have people on staff whose job description is to ride in planes all week, the air courier companies look for members of the general public to serve as their couriers. To entice people to perform this minimal service, the air courier companies offer them a discount on the fare.

Some misconceptions about air courier travel

Before I continue, let me clear up some misconceptions about air courier travel and allay any suspicions you may have. First of all, air courier shipments are perfectly legal and safe. As I mentioned earlier, they have been going on for decades. Over the years the air courier companies, the airlines, and customs agencies have worked together to develop policies and procedures that guarantee the safety and integrity of these shipments.

One result of these procedures is that the courier never actually handles the shipment. You *accompany* the shipment. You do not pick it up, carry it, or deliver it. Many times you will never even see the cargo you are accompanying. If you do see it, it will be when representatives of the courier company are either delivering it to the airline or collecting it at customs. It is extremely rare that the courier has physical contact with the shipment.

Likewise, the courier has no legal liability for anything being shipped by the courier company. You can answer the airline's questions about how you packed your bags truthfully because they refer only to your personal baggage. The airline knows you did not pack the courier shipment and that it is not *truly* your baggage. Everyone involved — the air courier company, the airline, the customs officials — merely acknowledges the polite fiction that this stuff is the passenger's baggage (i.e. your baggage) to allow the shipment to receive expedited handling.

Because the system has been designed to eliminate the courier as a variable, virtually anyone can be a courier. There are no tests, no background checks, no bonding procedures. As long as you are over 18 years of age, hold a valid passport, and are in good health, you can travel as an air courier.

Another major misconception about air courier travel is that it is invariably a last-minute affair — that you must provide the courier company your phone number and then be willing to dash off to points unknown whenever they call you. Not so. Air courier travel can be remarkably like "regular" travel. You can plan ahead, book on the phone, and very often pay for your trip right then and there with a credit card.

The peculiarities of air courier travel

That's not to say that air courier travel is *exactly* like regular travel. There are important differences, some of them quite wonderful and others that may take some getting used to.

- *The fare structure.* Air courier fares are like "regular" fares in that they rise and fall with the seasons. For example, it's more expensive to fly to Europe during the summer than it is in the winter, whether you're flying as a courier or not. However, the air courier fare structure is precisely the opposite of normal fares in one very important respect. As the date of the flight approaches, the fare goes down not up. Anyone who has had to travel at short notice knows how the airlines stick it to last-minute travelers. The air courier companies, however, have other concerns. They must have a courier on every flight or else they can't ship their cargo. In the worst case scenario, a courier company will put one of its employees on a flight to make sure the shipment goes through. They don't like to do that however, so as flight date approaches and the courier slot is still empty, or if they have a courier cancel, they get very nervous and drop the fare to attract a courier. It is these last-minute availabilities that produce truly enormous discounts and even free flights.

- **Baggage restrictions.** Many air courier companies restrict their couriers to carry-on luggage. They are, after all, using the passenger's normal luggage allotment for their freight. A growing number of air courier companies, however, especially those flying to the Far East, allow couriers to check at least one bag. Traveling light is a skill long since acquired by most business travelers. Others may find it a bit of an adjustment. I know I did when I first started flying as a courier. I quickly adjusted, however, and in fact found the experience quite liberating. It also produced some bona fide travel adventures. Doing laundry at home is an unpleasant chore; doing laundry in a strange country (as you inevitably must if you travel with one carry-on bag) is an adventure.
- **Limited gateways.** Air courier travel is an international phenomenon; there are no domestic courier flights, for obvious reasons. The courier business is concentrated in a few major "gateway cities," as I call them.

They are Montreal in Canada and, in the United States, New York, Miami, Chicago, San Francisco, and Los Angeles.

- *Solo travel.* The air courier company needs only one courier per flight since they can attach a virtually unlimited amount of cargo to that single ticket. If you want to travel with a friend you have several options. The best is to ask the air courier company to book the two of you on successive courier flights on successive days. That way you can depart and return a day apart. This is actually a travel strategy worth exploring whether you travel as a courier or not. Putting aside the dreadful thought of what happens in the unlikely event of a crash, traveling on successive days gives each person a day at the destination to do whatever they want without fear of boring or inconveniencing the other person.

- *Length of stay restrictions.* All courier flights are restricted in some way or another. Some flights have a fixed length of stay of 7 or 14 days. Sometimes the length of stay to a particular destination will be predetermined by the day of the week on which you leave. Other air courier companies let the courier pick the date of return, *subject to availability*, within a period of a month, three months, six months, or in extremely rare instances, a year. "Subject to availability" means that there is only one return seat available per day, so if someone else has already picked the 15th of the month as a return date you will have to choose another date. Nor can you change your ticket once booked, even if you are willing to pay an additional penalty fee. If you fall in love with Thailand and want to stay an extra week, too bad.

- *No ticket.* One of the weirdest aspects of air courier travel for most people is the fact that when you pay for your ticket, you don't actually get it. Instead, you must wait until the day of the flight, when you may have to meet someone you've never met at the airport to receive your ticket and get checked in. This adds a certain James Bond, cloak and dagger flavor that can be fun, but it is just as likely to make you nervous your first time around. Likewise, you usually won't receive your return ticket until shortly before your return flight.

The 'typical' air courier trip

First of all, no air courier trip will be exactly like another. Every air courier company has slightly different policies and procedures, so every experience will be slightly different. Nonetheless, in most cases, you can expect your air courier journey to unfold along these lines:

Step 1: Booking your flight

It's easy to book by phone. Simply call and say, "Hi. I'd like to go to Rio in June. What's available?" and they'll tell you. If you make a booking, you will have to pay for your trip as soon as possible. The seat is not officially yours until you pay and a delay in paying may mean losing the ticket.

Some companies will hold your reservation for a nonrefundable deposit, pending full payment by a certain number of days before departure. If there is a comfortable length of time before the flight, you may be able to pay by a personal check through the mail. More and more companies take credit cards (which may add several percent to the cost of your ticket). More common are policies that require payment in cash or by certified check as soon as possible. That can mean showing up in person or sending payment by overnight mail.

Once you have booked and secured a flight, you will most likely be asked to sign a contract. At this time, the company will make sure that you meet the minimum requirements (are 18 or 21 years of age, have a valid passport, don't have a spiked, day-glo hair-do and safety pins through your cheeks, and so forth). Sometimes all the contract signing can be handled by fax. In some cases, you won't be asked to sign anything until you are being checked aboard your flight.

Step 2: Boarding your flight

In the words of one air courier company, "you are not buying a ticket, but a trip." Even though your name may be on it, the ticket, technically, belongs to the air courier company. It's a subtle distinction that gives the courier company the right to "bump" you from the flight at the last minute. It does happen, but very, very infrequently.

Another result is that you will not receive the actual ticket until shortly before the flight. The day before the flight, you will most likely be required to check in by phone; they want to make sure you're still "on" for the trip. On the day of the flight, well before your scheduled departure time (two or three hours), you will meet a representative of the courier company at a prearranged location in the airport — or, less frequently, at the courier company's offices. Some companies will ask you to phone in when you get to the airline terminal.

Arriving at the airport with no ticket, often with rather vague instructions on where to meet someone you have never laid eyes on, is a new experience for most travelers. Frankly it can be a little nerve-wracking.

When the courier company rep arrives, you may be handed a one way ticket to your destination, a sealed envelope, or "pouch," containing the cargo manifests for the shipment you will accompany, and a sheet of instructions telling you what to do for the return flight. Of these three items, the only one you are certain to receive is the ticket. Many companies have developed systems for getting their shipments through without entrusting the manifest to the onboard courier. And on some runs, you will be "coming back empty," that is you will have no courier duties on the return trip and, hence, need do nothing more than show up for and board the return flight. In that case, you may receive your return ticket at this time.

The courier company representative will make sure that you are booked on the flight and get your boarding pass. In some cases, the rep will leave you in a waiting area and go deal with the ticket agents without you having to be present. At the very least, the courier company representative will be at your elbow as you go through the check-in procedure.

The same is true of the shipment you are accompanying. Many times you will never see the shipment you are accompanying; other times, the courier company rep will check in the pouches at the same time you are checked in. Several times I've watched burly cargo handlers drag large, heavy, corrugated plastic bags full of smaller parcels to the weighing machine at the airline counter, while I stood by. I have watched even larger loads being retrieved at my destinations (usually in the Far East). The point is, you will never be asked to physically manhandle the cargo yourself. You may be given the airline luggage check stubs for the courier shipment. If so, you will have to surrender them to the courier representative at your destination.

You will most likely be given something to help you identify yourself to the rep at the other end. One English company asks you to fill out a short questionnaire describing your dress and physical appearance; this is then faxed to the receiving company. Some companies issue their couriers colored lapel pins or laminated, clip-on plastic ID tags, similar to those worn by airport personnel. Another courier company gives its onboard couriers a pin-on button that says, "COURIER. WHERE'S THE SHIP'S OFFICE?" (The ship's office is a term that refers to the customs office. It dates from the times when most international cargo traveled by sea.) I have even been given a sticker with the words "On-Board Courier" in Chinese. Generally, your manifest envelope will serve as your identification. These are usually large, white, plastic envelopes with the courier company name or "ON-BOARD COURIER POUCH" emblazoned on them.

Your major responsibility en route is to keep the manifests, the baggage claim stubs, and your instruction sheet safe and secure about your person. Hardly an onerous task.

Step 3: Arriving at your destination

When you arrive at your destination, you will be met by another representative of the air courier company. You may have been instructed to hold up the envelope containing the manifests as you leave the customs area to identify you to the person meeting your flight. Sometimes you will be given a phone number to call when you have cleared through customs. (Usually you will breeze through customs by following the "Nothing To Declare" signs.)

Once you make contact with the receiving courier company, you will be asked to wait — in the customs area of the terminal or in a building elsewhere on the airport grounds — while the courier company representative walks the paperwork and the checked baggage through the customs process. Once that's done, you'll be free to leave. In my experience, this has been a hassle-free experience. On other trips, I haven't even been required to wait around; the rep simply asked where they could get in touch with me if they had to and let me go.

Once through customs, you are on your own, free to do and see as you please until the return flight.

Step 4: Returning home

I have found that one of the most important documents I carry as a courier is the instruction sheet for my return flight. By all means, keep this document in a safe place. I copy the key information — return flight number and date, contact name, and phone numbers — onto several different pieces of paper to stash in various wallets and shirt pockets, just in case.

Usually, you will be asked to check in by phone with the local office of the air courier company several days before your return flight to confirm your flight and pick up any last minute instructions or changes in plan. And don't forget to call or think it's just a formality that can be skipped. I have had flight times switched at the last minute. So always remember to check in. At the very least, failure to check in will earn a black mark by your name in the courier company's records.

On the day of your return flight, the arrangements are usually a mirror image of the routine on the flight out — meet the representative at the airport, receive the manifests, if any, get checked in, receive your ticket, board the flight, meet the representative back in New York or wherever. Most courier company reps will speak English, but you cannot always expect your foreign contact to speak, let alone be fluent in, English. Fortunately, unless you have some problem, the procedure is so cut-and-dried that not being able to speak the language won't be a handicap. Also, if there is likely to be a language barrier, the courier company may very well provide you with bilingual materials. I have been given instructions and explanations in Japanese, Chinese, and Thai on various courier trips.

That's all there is to it. Considering how much you save on your fare, it's extremely well paid "employment."

How good a deal is it?

In the good old days (which means about 20 years ago) air courier travel was free. In fact, some companies even paid for some of the courier's expenses. In the eighties, however, courier companies learned that they could charge a modest fare and still get takers. Ever since, air courier fares have been creeping closer and closer to consolidator fares and even coming perilously close in some cases to the airlines' published fares. Recently, the number of courier flights and destinations began to drop off sharply. Meanwhile a number of self-styled air courier "associations" continued to market air courier travel as the same super bargain it was ten years ago. The result was that more and more couriers were chasing fewer and fewer flights, which further encouraged the courier companies to raise fares.

Today it takes a keen eye to distinguish the real air courier bargains. Just because it's advertised as a courier flight doesn't mean you're getting the best possible deal. Always check courier fares against consolidator fares to the same destination. This is especially true if you have to travel to a gateway city from elsewhere.

Obviously, the first step in recognizing a bargain is knowing what an item "should" cost. That's easy enough to do by calling the airlines. You may also want to call a few consolidators to see what they're offering. You might also consult *Jax Fax* magazine (see Chapter Ten). Determining the "going rate" is especially important if you don't live in or near one of the courier gateway cities.

I would also urge you to bear in mind some of the tradeoffs involved in courier travel. If a consolidator flight, say, is just $30 more, ask yourself if having a full luggage allotment and some added flexibility in picking dates might be worth that extra bit of money. On the other hand, consolidator tickets often involve "off-brand" foreign airlines whereas air courier companies typically use major carriers, so factor that in as well.

All that being said, most courier fares represent a decent discount off the typical "supersaver" fares offered by the airlines. Here is a sort of worst-case example from my personal experience. I was traveling to London in October. I had made social and business commitments so I had little flexibility as to dates and couldn't risk waiting for a last-minute discount. I decided to book a courier flight well in advance — three months — which meant I would be paying the highest courier fare. Nonetheless, I was able to book a flight for $250 roundtrip, including taxes. A low-fare search on the Internet the same day turned up a fare quote of $420 (plus a $28 departure tax). Closer to flight time, I would have been able to get a published fare of $298 (again, plus a $28 departure tax). Consolidator fares were slightly higher than the courier fare I had paid.

I should also note that fares from New York tend to be higher anyway and London is by far the most popular courier destination and, therefore, the destination with the highest courier fares. You can typically expect to get much deeper discounts on other routes and from other gateways.

The one situation in which courier travel offers a clear-cut, plain as the nose on your face fare difference is in the case of last-minute availabilities. Then the fares can be as low as 30% of the regular fare and they might even be free. Free flights and super-discounts are rarest out of New York (New Yorkers are a tough bunch) and most frequent from the West Coast (Californians are a mellow bunch).

Obviously, chasing last-minute courier fares is not for everyone. Those who have limited vacation time, for which they must plan well in advance, cannot take a chance on a last-minute flight being available. However, for many people the peculiarities of courier fare structures offer a superb opportunity. You may be one of them, especially if you are adventurous enough to take whatever destination presents itself when you call.

Preeminent in this group are retirees who not only have the time but very often a yen to travel as well. Air courier companies, for their part, love working with older couriers; they find them to be far more reliable than their sometimes flighty (no pun intended) youthful counterparts. Others who can benefit from last-minute courier fares are freelancers and those whose schedules are unpredictable. Students, too, are frequent couriers since they are often not too fussy about where they go, just so long as they go there. Businesspeople should not dismiss courier travel out of hand. I know of businesspeople with a regular need to visit certain destinations who take advantage of attractively priced courier opportunities when they arise. Also, if you suddenly have to get to, say, Hong Kong tomorrow, pick up a phone and call a courier company that flies there. The odds are against finding a flight for the next day, but if you do the fare will be a bargain you'll brag about for years to come.

Courier contacts

What follows is a listing of air courier companies (and a few courier booking agencies) in the United States and Canada. I have included only the most important information here.

The number of courier destinations has been shrinking rapidly in the last year or so, but some cities may reappear. Since most courier companies serve a single broad area (Asia, South America, etc.), you may want to call just in case they are offering a destination not mentioned here.

The list is organized geographically, from north to south and east to west, beginning with Montreal and ending with Los Angeles. The fares and destinations cited are subject to change, often on a month to month basis.

Before you contact any courier company, reread this chapter carefully. Remember that these companies are in the freight business, not the passenger business. They have limited patience with "dumb" questions.

MONTREAL

F.B. On-Board Courier Service
5110 Fairway Street
Lachine, Quebec H8T 1B8
(514) 631-2677
Destination: London ($525-$625 CDN)

Departure can also be from **Toronto**, but booking must be made through the Montreal office. F.B.'s **Vancouver** office, (604) 278-1266, also has flights to Hong Kong for about $700 CDN.

NEW YORK

New York is without a doubt the air courier capital of the United States. No other gateway city comes close, either in terms of the number of companies booking onboard couriers or the number of destinations served.

There are four booking agencies in the New York area: Air-Tech, As You Like It, Marathon, and Now Voyager. While there is a good bit of overlap in their listings, they don't offer precisely the same flights, and at any given time one may be sitting on a last-minute special that the other doesn't know about. So you may find it worth your while to check with all of them to see what they are offering. Booking agents usually charge a small premium over the fare you would be quoted when dealing with the courier company itself.

Air Cargo Partners (ACP)
149-32 132nd Street
JFK International Airport
Jamaica, NY 11430
(888) VEX-MOVE (839-6683); (718) 529-6814, ext. 201
Destination: London ($249-$660)

ACP is the in-house courier operation of Virgin Atlantic Cargo. It offers three courier departures daily, two from JFK and one from nearby Newark. In my opinion, its fares are too high to make it truly attractive to couriers. On the plus side: fares include the departure tax, ACP lets you check bags, and there is no minimum stay, making London an option for a long weekend

ACP also operates London courier flights from **Boston**,

Los Angeles, Miami, Orlando, San Francisco, and **Washington, DC.** All flights must be booked through ACP's New York office. In addition, you can call ACP for discounted tickets from these cities to Athens, Hong Kong, Johannesburg, Kuala Lumpur, and Tokyo. These are not courier slots, so more than one person can book on the same flight.

Air Facility
153-40 Rockaway Boulevard
Jamaica, NY 11434
(718) 712-1769
Destinations: Buenos Aires ($400–$480), Montevideo ($300–$480), Rio de Janeiro ($300–$480), Sao Paulo ($200–$480)

This is an extremely friendly and helpful operation that offers some very attractive fares. Prices rise sharply, however, at Christmas time. You can book up to two months in advance. Last-minute flights are typically $100 less than the posted fare.

The length of stay varies with the day of departure from 7 to 15 days. Be aware, too, that trips to Brazil require a tourist visa for U.S. citizens; obtaining the visa is the courier's responsibility. Air Facility also has an office in **Miami**.

Air-Tech Ltd.
588 Broadway
Suite 204
New York, NY 10012
(212) 219-7000, ext. 206
www.airtech.com

Air-Tech specializes in space-available travel and is covered elsewhere in this book (see Chapter Two). However, they book courier flights as a sideline and offer the flights of most New York area courier companies.

Not all destinations are available at all times, however, and there is only one flight a day to Australia; it allows the courier to terminate at any one (but only one) of the four destination cities, Brisbane, Cairns, Melbourne, and Sydney. Air-Tech occasionally has last-minute specials to offer.

As You Like It Travel
224 West 35th Street
Suite 1126
New York, NY 10001
(212) 216-0644
www.asulikeit.com

This booking agent brings years of experience to the air courier market and seems to offer extremely competitive fares to the destinations it offers. There is no application fee and they will hold a reservation for 24 hours for New York residents and for three days for others, pending payment in full by cash, money order, or credit card. No personal checks. Bookings can be made up to three months in advance. Recent last-minute specials included Dublin or Mexico City for $150 roundtrip and London for $199. As You Like it also sells consolidator tickets and will help you get a discounted ticket for a companion on your courier flight.

Courier Network
515 West 29th Street
New York, NY 10001
(212) 947-3738
Destination: Tel Aviv, Israel ($500–$700)

Courier Network flies from New York to Tel Aviv, Israel. Book early; this is a very popular route. Your stay in Israel can range from two weeks to two months. You are allowed one checked piece of luggage in addition to your carry-on allotment.

East–West Express
149–35 177th Street
Jamaica, NY 11434
(718) 656-6246
Destinations: Auckland ($1000–$1300), Bangkok ($600–$800), Beijing ($600–$800), Brisbane ($1000–$1400), Cairns ($1000–$1400), Capetown ($900–$1200), Hong Kong ($600–$800), Johannesburg ($900–$1200), Manila ($600–$800), Melbourne ($1000–$1400), Seoul ($600–$800), Shanghai ($600–$800), Singapore ($600–$800), Sydney ($1000–$1400), Taipei ($600–$800),

Tokyo ($600–$800)

The Australia run is a single flight out of New York, which requires a visa and allows the courier to choose Sydney, Melbourne, Brisbane, or Cairns as the final destination. It makes a stop in **Los Angeles**, and the courier can originate there. It's first-come, first-served, so if an LA courier books a flight on a given day, that day's run is not available to a courier in New York, and vice versa. All of East-West's Asian destinations make connecting flights in Tokyo, but none allows a stopover. All flights restrict the courier to carry-on luggage only on the outbound leg. Runs to Australia and South Africa allow the courier to check two bags on the return trip. You can book up to two months in advance and stay for up to 30, 60, or 90 days. Check East-West's fares against consolidators' before making a booking decision.

Global Delivery Systems
147-05 176th Street
Jamaica, NY 11434
(718) 995-2708
Destinations: Amsterdam ($300–$500), Bangkok ($600–$800), Brussels ($300–$550), Copenhagen ($300–$600), Hong Kong ($500–$800), London ($250–$450), Madrid ($378–$678), Manila ($500–$800), Milan ($350–$750), Paris ($328–$578), Rome ($328–$728), Singapore ($278–$800), Tokyo ($428–$800)

Global Delivery Systems is strictly a wholesaler. That is, it ships cargo for other companies that ship it for customers like you and me. Quoted fares include a $28 departure tax. Most destinations now have a flexible stay of up to three months. That means that, subject to availability, you can pick your own date of return within that window.

Generally, you can expect to book your flight three to six weeks in advance, but flights are sometimes available on shorter notice. Global requires a $100 return-guarantee deposit by personal check and has a strict carry-on only policy; the exception is London, to which Global allows a full luggage allotment.

Johnny Air Cargo
69-04 Roosevelt Avenue

Woodside, NY 11377
(718) 397-5099
Destination: Manila ($299-$899)

Fares are highest during holiday periods. The stay is ten days to two months and Johnny requires a $250 return-guarantee deposit. Couriers must be between 18 and 55 years old. Book at least two months in advance; four or more months in advance for busy periods like December. Johnny also offers courier flights to Manila from **Los Angeles** and **San Francisco**.

Jupiter Air, Ltd.
Building #14
JFK International Airport
Jamaica, NY 11430
(718) 656-6050
Destination: Hong Kong ($400-$600)

You can courier one way to Hong Kong. The one way fare is one half the roundtrip fare. Couriers also pay a $7 airport tax and must provide a $100 return-guarantee deposit (more on some runs), which Jupiter refunds promptly after your return. Last-minute specials are sometimes available.

Most of Jupiter's runs are strictly carry-on only, unless you are staying more than three weeks, in which case you are allowed one checked piece of luggage. Flights can be booked six weeks to two months in advance. First-time couriers pay a $35 "initiation fee," which is good for five years and is valid for travel from any of Jupiter's U.S. locations. Jupiter also operates courier service from **Los Angeles** and **San Francisco**.

Now Voyager
74 Varick Street
Suite 307
New York, NY 10013
(212) 431-1616
www.nowvoyagertravel.com

Now Voyager, New York's oldest courier booking agency has been de-emphasizing courier travel recently. It no longer charges a $50 annual registration fee. In most cases, there will be a

$100 return-guarantee deposit in the form of a personal check, which will be destroyed upon your return. All flights are nonrefundable once paid for.

Now Voyager offers special non-courier flights to selected international destinations and you can also get discounted domestic tickets on "eight minor to major airlines."

World Courier, Inc.
1313 4th Avenue
New Hyde Park, NY 11040
(516) 354-2600
Destination: Mexico City ($100-$200)

World Courier is an air courier retailer. That means it offers expedited cargo services exclusively to its own roster of business clients. It allows couriers to check one bag of up to 40 pounds. You can stay seven days in Mexico City.

MIAMI

Miami is a major courier hub to South and Central America. The selection of available destinations changes frequently; at one time or another, every major city in Latin America has been reachable from Miami, along with European destinations like London and Madrid. It's not a bad idea to check in regularly with the companies listed below to see what's currently available.

Air Facility
2460 NW 66th Avenue
Building 701, Suite A-270
Miami, FL 33122
(305) 871-4990
Destinations: Buenos Aires ($425-$525), Rio de Janeiro ($350)

One way trips are available for $400 to Buenos Aires and full fare to Rio. The flight to Rio requires U.S. citizens to travel with a business visa. Air Facility will provide the courier with a letter, which must then be presented to a Brazilian consulate in order to obtain a visa. The consulate in Miami has been charging about $100 for such a visa. See the **New York** listing for more policy information. Flights can be booked up to two months in advance.

International Bonded Couriers, Inc. (IBC)
8401 NW 17th Street
Miami, FL 33126-1009
(305) 591-8080
Destinations: Buenos Aires ($450), Santiago ($450)

IBC uses onboard freelance couriers from time to time. No return-guarantee deposit is required, and there are also no last-minute fare reductions. Flights can be booked only two or three weeks in advance. Couriers are limited to carry-on luggage and the stay is limited to seven days.

Trans-Air Systems, Inc.
7264 NW 25th Street
Miami, FL 33122
(305) 592-1771
Destinations: Guatemala City ($280-$300), Quito ($250-$300)

Stays of up to a year can be obtained for higher fares. One way trips are available for $250-$300. Bookings can be made up to two months in advance, three months in advance for December.

CHICAGO

Courier service from Chicago has been curtailed drastically in recent years, as major companies like Jupiter and Global Delivery Systems withdrew from the market. However, one start-up company is trying to buck the trend.

Synergy Worldwide Delivery, Inc.
2660 Greenleaf Avenue
Elk Grove Village, IL 60007
(877) 742-7934

(847) 439-9429
Destinations: London, Brussels

At press time, schedules were erratic and fares had not been finalized. Luggage restrictions apparently vary according to the flight.

SAN FRANCISCO

Johnny Air Cargo
37 Saint Francis Square
Daly City CA 94015
(650) 991-7080
Destination: Manila ($350-$700)

The highest fares are for holiday periods such as Christmas. Couriers can book up to two months in advance, stay up to three months, are restricted to carry-on baggage only in both directions, and must leave a $250 return-guarantee deposit.

Johnny also operates courier service from **New York** and **Los Angeles**. See the **New York** listing for policy information.

Jupiter Air, Ltd.
811 Sneath Lane
San Bruno, CA 94066
(650) 635-1700
Ext. 216
Destinations: Manila ($405-$455), Singapore ($350-$500)

All couriers must provide a $250 return-guarantee deposit on the Manila run, $100 for Singapore. Couriers are allowed one checked bag on the Singapore run and two on the Manila run. Jupiter also operates courier flights from **Los Angeles** and **New York**.

See the **New York** listing for more on its fees and policies.

UTL Travel
320 Corey Way
South San Francisco, CA 94080
(650) 583-5074

Destinations: Manila ($455-$535), Singapore ($400-$535)

Fares will be higher during the summer and at Christmas time. UTL will offer reduced fares if there is a last-minute need for couriers; the fare varies, but it is usually in the $250 range. All runs require a $100 return-guarantee deposit, which is returned to you automatically by mail on your return. You can stay for one week to 30 days. Baggage restrictions vary by destination and carrier.

LOS ANGELES

East-West Express
(*see New York*)
Destinations: Auckland ($750-$1000), Brisbane ($750-$1200), Cairns ($750-$1200), Melbourne ($750-$1200), Sydney ($750-$1200)

East-West Express offers one courier run from LAX to Australia and New Zealand and offers the courier a choice of final destination. The run originates in New York and stops in LA, so the courier can board in either city. An Australian visa is required. All flights must be booked and paid for through the **New York** office. See that listing for more details.

Johnny Air Cargo
203 South Vermont Avenue
Los Angeles, CA 90004
(213) 386-7080
Destination: Manila ($475-$850)

Holiday periods are the most expensive. Stays of two or three months are possible. You serve as a courier in both directions, are restricted to carry-on luggage only, and must leave a $250 return-guarantee deposit. Johnny also operates courier runs from **New York** and **San Francisco**. See the **New York** listing for policy information.

Jupiter Air, Ltd.
460 South Hindry Avenue
Unit D

Burlingame, CA 94010
(650) 697-7892
Destinations: Bangkok ($400-$450), Hong Kong ($400-$500),
Seoul ($350-$400), Singapore ($400-$500)

If you are available to fly at the last minute and they have an
opening, Jupiter will reduce its fares by 50% or more. Flights
from LA allow carry-on luggage only. You must provide a $200
return-guarantee deposit. Jupiter also operates courier service
out of **New York** and **San Francisco**. See the **New York** listing
for more details on Jupiter's policies and procedures.

Chapter Eight

Using the Internet

One of the most pernicious myths in circulation today is that the best — perhaps the only — way to get the absolutely cheapest air fare is to go on the Internet. I'm not sure what makes this myth so tenacious. Maybe it's the airlines. They'd love nothing more than to tear customers away from travel agents and sit them down in front of computer screens where the airlines could control the information they receive. Maybe it's the press, which seems all aswoon with the romance of life on the Information Superhighway. But one thing I know for certain: It just ain't so.

That's not to say that you cannot find great deals on the Internet — sometimes. But the syllogism "I booked my ticket on the Internet, therefore I got the best fare" just doesn't withstand scrutiny. A 1998 study by Penn State professor Arvind Rangaswamy found that, due in part to the many options served up by online booking services, customers became confused and often wound up spending more than they intended. Much of the anecdotal evidence seems to back him up.

Preview Travel, an Internet travel agency that was recently purchased by Travelocity (see below), drew a great deal of flak from the travel agent community with a series of radio advertisements that ridiculed the very idea of dealing with a travel agent. The ads suggested, none too subtly, that logging on to Preview Travel would not only offer the customer better service but better fares. One travel agent was so incensed that he put Preview to the test and discovered that on a typical midweek business-trip booking, his agents were able to beat Preview's fare by $200 — *on exactly the same flights.*

Terry Trippler, an industry observer who has made a career of puncturing myths about air fares, cites the example of an international trip booked on an airline's own web site. The "lowest" Washington-Cairo fare quoted by the online booking engine was $2,412.33. A call to a travel agent turned up a fare of $961.33, a saving of over 60% — *on exactly the same flights.*

What's going on here? Are the online booking engines and the airlines' own web sites setting out in a cold and calculating fashion to lie to us and rob us blind? Not really. There are a number of factors at work, starting with the computer programs that power these online booking engines. They are written to be efficient and, therefore, follow a line-of-least-resistance logic. "If this, then that," they say to themselves and not "If this, then maybe there are three or four things I should try out." That programming results, for example, in an airline's own "Lowest Fare" search option reacting to a request for a Seattle-Miami ticket by routing the passenger through Atlanta when a change in Cincinnati would result in, not only a lower fare, but a shorter trip. A savvy travel agent will know that but a computer's just too dumb.

So even with the best intentions in the world, an online booking system may fall short of the goal. But what if the creators of the system decide that there are some things it won't let you do? In that case, you're out of luck. An airline's own site, for example, is certainly not going to tell you about lower fares available from other airlines, even from their code-share "partners." If whoever creates the site decides not to include a space in which to enter the passengers' ages, you will never learn about any senior discount to which you may be entitled. If the programmers decide not to feed in information about promotional fares, you will not be alerted to their existence. Some of these omissions are obviously deliberate, others may be oversights; the result is the same: you don't get the best fare.

Another problem is that computers are at the mercy of the information fed into them. An online booking engine may try to give you the best fare for the dates and times you gave it, but it will not "think" to suggest that you could get a lower fare by leaving a few hours or a day earlier. And it certainly won't think to suggest an alternate routing. And no online booking engine that I know of will allow you to enter a known fare code to come up with an itinerary on which that fare would be valid. (See Ploy #6 in Chapter One.)

But don't turn off your browser just yet. For all its faults and pitfalls, the Internet remains a cornucopia of information. Used wisely, it will provide you with good information and the occasional bona fide bargain.

Web specials

Perhaps the best air fare deals to be found on the Internet are the "web specials" which virtually every airline now offers. Most of them will even e-mail you a weekly list of tempting bargains.

The typical web special is posted on the airline's web site on Wednesday and involves travel for the coming weekend, with travel beginning on Friday or Saturday and returning Sunday, Monday, or Tuesday. Most, but not all, of these trips will be departing from one of the airline's main hubs. Trips like these may not be to everyone's taste; but if you have family or friends in a city on the list, or just have a hankering to visit places you might otherwise overlook, they could be just the ticket.

Some airlines have gone beyond the weekend trip formula to offer special deals to select international and domestic destinations. American Airlines has even taken to posting special deals on an irregular and unpredictable basis.

You can log on to an airline's web site once a week to browse the specials, but most people opt to have the airlines e-mail them a weekly heads-up. Signing up is simple; just go to the airline's web site and you will find a simple form in which to enter your e-mail address. Obviously, you will want to get information for the airlines that fly from your local airport, and if you live in or near a major hub, you will most definitely want to be on that airline's mailing list. But there's nothing stopping you from signing up for every airline offering these specials. If you'd rather not have your electronic mailbox cluttered with messages from individual airlines, *Best Fares* magazine compiles this information on its web site (www.bestfares.com).

Priceline

www.priceline.com

"Name your own price for an airline ticket!" Has a nice ring to it, doesn't it? That's the pitch used by Priceline.com, an Internet company that has reaped a windfall of publicity with its "patented" business model that lets you log on to its web site and bid on an airline ticket. You pick the city pairs and the dates, name your best price, and wait to see if Priceline accepts your bid. If it does, you are committed to buying the ticket whether you actually take the trip or not. At first glance, it seems like a terrific deal. After all, you might reason, an airline will be happy to sell me a seat for $39 that might otherwise go empty.

The reality seems to be something else again. Although Priceline is close-mouthed about not only its business methods but also the results of its auctions, it seems that there are few real bargains to be had here. You place your bid and then Priceline, through some undisclosed process, finds out if they can meet it. Most of the time, and especially if you have submitted a low-ball bid, you will be unsuccessful. I have seen very little evidence that Priceline produces a fare lower than the lowest published fare for the route in question on a regular basis. (There have been reports that Priceline will sometimes sell a ticket at a loss.) There is even less evidence that Priceline can consistently beat consolidator fares.

A major catch is that when Priceline accepts your bid, it adds taxes, fees, and service charges which can increase your effective fare by as much as 30 percent! A more accurate slogan would be "Name your own price — but never get it."

There's a lot more fine print (which many people never bother reading) that can result in flights leaving at the crack of dawn or late at night, bizarre routings with multiple plane changes, and so forth. Tickets are completely non-changeable, even by the airline. So if you find your return flight leaving before the rental car office opens, you're stuck.

Another problem with Priceline is that it is not a true auction. In other words, you cannot keep raising your bid until you buy what you want. If your initial bid fails, you get the message "If you would like to submit a second request for this trip there is a $25 nonrefundable service charge."

The result is that Priceline has its detractors, including *Consumer Reports Travel Letter*, which found nothing but problems with the system — so much so that it finally gave up on trying to book a trip. Other complaints I've seen posted on the Internet by angry customers include Priceline failing to inform passengers when the airline changes the flight schedule, not living up to its own terms and conditions, and sending the wrong ticket and then refusing to exchange it. Taxes and undisclosed fees can wind up making the Priceline fare more expensive than one booked through a travel agent. If you'd like to see a fairly typical Priceline complaint, visit http://www.california.com/~rpcman/priceline.html.

As that story indicates, complaining seems to do little good. Priceline's customer service department has become legendary (or infamous) for its lack of response. One customer even claims that a Priceline customer service rep told her, "Sue us!"

In spite of all this, some people apparently get deals they like on Priceline. One result posted on an Internet newsgroup was a $200 roundtrip ticket from Washington, DC, to London on Icelandair. I have also heard of people getting good deals on hotels through Priceline's hotel auction.

Actually, you have to hand it to Priceline. They've used twenty-first century technology to create a sixteenth century marketplace, where the customer is always in the dark and always wrong, where the merchant holds all the cards, and where "bait and switch" has been raised to an art form. Currently, Priceline sells about 80,000 tickets a week. On top of it all, Wall Street and the media love them. Just goes to show what happens when Captain Kirk is your spokesman.

Winning the Priceline game

If, in spite of everything you've just read, you still want to try Priceline, here are some guidelines that may save you from becoming a victim.

- **Know the rules.** Before doing anything with Priceline, print out their instructions and terms and conditions and read them very carefully. Don't kid yourself that the worst-case scenario can't happen to you.
- **Never use Priceline for short trips.** Priceline's tendency to use late-late night and early-early morning flights can turn a relaxing three-day getaway into a sleep-deprived 30-hour stay at your destination.
- **Have a high threshold of pain.** Know going in that your trip (in either or both directions) may become a grueling marathon thanks to multiple stopovers and plane changes. Of course, you could luck out and get a direct flight.
- **Know the lowest published fare.** Perhaps the best situation in which to use Priceline is when you have to take a trip but the advance-purchase time has expired. (But first check other discount ticket sources to make sure they don't have what you're after.) Use a booking engine (see below) to determine the lowest advance-purchase fare on the route. Then bid somewhere around that fare (bearing in mind that Priceline will add up to 30 percent to your bid).
- **Fiddle with dates and airports.** You can't bid on the same itinerary more than once, but you can change dates and airports. Remember (see Chapter Two) that if you're flying from Los Angeles to New York you can leave from Ontario and fly to Newark, or from Burbank to Islip. If you're looking to bag a great fare for a vacation far in the future, you can probably be flexible with both dates and destinations.
- **Self insure.** By this I mean know that Priceline is always a gamble and be prepared to lose all your money. If they send you the wrong ticket, for example, chances are you're screwed. If you can't afford to take that chance, don't.

Other web auctions

Priceline may have a lock on point-to-point air, but it isn't the only game in town. A growing number of sites offer a similar service. If you want to try your luck, here are some other online ticket auction promoters.

Sky Auction (www.skyauction.com)
> Here you bid on specific travel products, that are arranged geographically or by category. Although some air fare-only deals are available, most of the bidding is for resort stays and tour packages. This is a real auction, in which you compete against other bidders.

Travelfacts Auctions (www.bid4travel.com)
> Similar to Sky Auction. Mostly resorts and cruises.

Travel Auction Network (www.goinggoinggone.com) and *Travel Clearing House* (www.travelclearinghouse.com)
> These two seem to be related and linked to Calparrio International Travel (www.calparrio.com), a travel agency. The air fare deals they auction appear to be unsold seats on charters.

Airline-run auctions

Priceline may be trying to become the 900-pound gorilla in the Internet airline auction business, but there are other, quieter, players — the airlines themselves. These auctions are not ongoing affairs. Rather they come and go on an unpredictable basis. Among the airlines that have used this technique are Lufthansa (www.lufthansa.de), Martinair (www.martinairusa.com), Virgin Express (www.virgin-express.com), and South African Airways (www.saa.co.za). Martinair has auctioned seats from Florida to Amsterdam, but the others have been for flights originating abroad.

One of the more consistent cyber-auctioneers is Cathay Pacific (www.cathay-usa.com). You must register as a Cathay Pacific "Cyber Traveller" to gain access to auction information, but registration carries benefits such as Internet-only deals on things like Cathay's All Asia Pass (see Chapter Five).

You are much more likely to find a true bargain at an airline-run auction. In fact, Virgin Express once accepted a bid of 39 Irish pence for one of its flights! Unfortunately, finding current airline-run auctions can be a bit tricky. Your best bet is probably one of the Internet search engines, but you may have to wade through dozens of pages before you find what you're looking for — if then.

The Empire strikes back

The airlines, taking notice of Priceline's success, have decided to try to muscle in on its territory. According to reports in the trade press, six major airlines have taken a minority interest in Hotwire.com, sometimes code-named Purple Demon, a site that will sell tickets on all airlines.

The business model is different from Priceline's "name your own price" come on. At Hotwire, travelers will enter city pairs and dates, but not fares. The system will query airlines and then get back to them with a fare offer that, it is claimed, will represent a "substantial savings" over published fares.

The site was not operational at press time and it may change its name before launch, but the URL http://www.hotwire.com should get you there.

Internet booking engines

More and more people are actually purchasing airline tickets on the Internet, using what have come to be known as "booking engines," a term derived from "search engines," those ubiquitous guides to the Web that search out web sites based on keywords you type in. And indeed booking engines and search engines operate on similar principles. A booking engine is a powerful computer program with an interface that you can access via the Internet. When you go to a booking engine's web site, you will find some sort of form in which you can enter your origination and destination cities, travel dates, preferred travel times, number of passengers, and so forth. Most of them let you rank your preferences for things such as lowest fare, best routing, or flights closest to the times you specified. The computer program then searches its database of available flights and seats and comes up with a selection of flights and itineraries from which you can choose. With a credit card, the deal can be consummated online and your ticket will be mailed to you or, as is increasingly the case, you will be sent an e-mail message with the details of your ticketless travel arrangements.

There are two major types of web sites to which you can go to book air travel:

- *Airline web sites.* These provide information about and ticketing for the flights of that airline and no others.
- *Commercial web sites.* These are, in effect, travel agencies on the web and they include the big sites like Expedia, Travelocity, 1 Travel, and such. They offer information about, and ticketing for, a considerable number of different airlines.

These commercial sites like to present themselves as an alternative (a superior alternative at that) to your local travel agent, but the fact of the matter is they are travel agencies themselves. And as travel agents, they suffer from the squeeze plays being used by the airlines. When the airlines announced a $10 commission cap on all online bookings, the Internet agencies squealed just as loudly as the storefront travel agents they like to disparage.

In addition to the major online travel agencies, there are any number of smaller fry. Some of them are the online "branches" of storefront travel agencies. Others operate as affiliates of the major online travel agencies.

It all adds up to a lot of sites, but the powerful computer databases that underpin all these sites — the actual "engines" of the booking engines — are provided by a relative handful of vendors. The result is that you will see some startling similarities in "look and feel" as you browse from site to site.

Major online travel agencies

Most of the major commercial booking engines do pretty much the same thing in pretty much the same way, with individual differences that will probably lead you to prefer one over the others — assuming of course that you "test drive" them all.

The most important thing they do, as far as our discussion here is concerned, is allow you to book and buy airline tickets. Most of them also let you book rental cars and hotels. Some offer complete vacation packages and links to travel-related vendors and resources. All of this is accomplished online, with no human interaction. You pay by credit card through a system that encrypts your precious credit card information to protect it from those legions of sex-starved, pimply-faced, socially maladroit young men who, we all know, spend their every waking hour in windowless basement rooms wreaking havoc on other people's computers.

Seriously though, these systems are safe. There may be reasons not to book on the Internet (see below), but the fear of having your credit card number swiped is not one of them.

All of the online travel sites require you to register in order to use the system. Some ask for your credit card information up front. Registering doesn't obligate you in any way, but it does allow them to keep track of your visits. Once you have registered, the site may place a "cookie" on your hard drive. This is a little piece of computer code that lets the site recognize you when you return. It saves you the trouble of registering on each visit but it annoys (or scares) some people. You can set your browser to refuse cookies if you wish. This will slow you down considerably when logging on to some sites but it will give you the satisfaction of having poked Big Brother in the eye.

So which online agency should you use? A good plan is to choose an itinerary or two, perhaps one with which you are familiar, perhaps one you'd like to take. Then try them out on several of these services to see, first, how easy they are to use and, second, how they stack up in terms of giving you the best deal. Another tip: time your sessions on each site. You'll obviously get faster the more experience you have with online booking, but I think you'll be surprised at how long it takes to book a complete air-car-hotel trip. Compare this to the amount of time it would take to call a travel agent, who knows your likes and dislikes, and request a package (see Ploy #4 in Chapter One).

Gomez Advisors (www.gomez.com), which bills itself as the "e-commerce authority," rates the big online travel agencies once a quarter, according to their usefulness to business, leisure, and budget (that's us) travelers. In addition to posting consumer feedback on the sites, Gomez also has a helpful feature that lets you compare two booking engines head to head.

My personal bias is that the online booking engines may be a good place to book domestic tickets (assuming you know a good fare deal when you see it), but they are seldom your best choice for international travel. A consolidator will almost always be able to beat published fares for overseas trips.

Here, then, are some of the major online travel agencies. I have limited my discussion to those features that I found most interesting, but I encourage you to log on and explore them for yourself. All of them offer many more bells and whistles than are covered here, everything from online guidebooks to chat rooms.

Expedia

www.expedia.msn.com

Microsoft's campaign to own the entire world continues with this online travel agency, which has some nice features. If your trip is a straightforward roundtrip, you can use the "Express Search" on the front page to get a quick reading for the city pair and dates of your choice.

My favorite is the "Fare Compare" section that lets you search for the lowest published fares for a given city pair. When you do, you are presented with a list of fares, the airlines offering them, and a place to click to see the detailed fare rules accompanying the fare. This is often likely to turn up a fare that's lower than the one you get when you enter the same cities in the Express Search. Why? Because the cheaper fare might not be available on the dates you selected or you might have to use a creative routing. Unfortunately, you cannot go from the fare or fare code to a list of flights on which it will work. You are directed to turn to the "Flight Wizard," the more complete booking engine, and use the parameters laid out in the fare code in an effort to find an itinerary that will work.

Another nice feature is Price Matcher, which is a Priceline-like bidding system. As with Priceline, you commit to prepayment but unlike your Priceline bid, your Expedia bid includes all taxes and extras and Expedia will charge you a lower fare than you bid if they find one. The "Fare Tracker" feature is a weekly e-mail alert that will tell you the best fares on three routes of your choice.

In a move that some people see as quintessentially Gatesian, Expedia has announced that it will bar entry to its site to people who continually browse but never buy. I suspect, however, that you would have to do far more browsing than any sane person is likely to do before incurring this dire penalty.

LowestFare.com

www.lowestfare.com

This site is affiliated with Global Discount Travel Services of Las Vegas, the company that is unloading Carl Icahn's excess inventory of TWA tickets (see Chapter Two). Consequently, it is a good place to book discounted TWA tickets online, although you can make a booking on any airline. The site also features special deals and discounts on leisure travel, like $15-a-night midweek hotel stay in Las Vegas, with no limit placed on the amount of money you can lose in the casino!

Travelocity

www.travelocity.com

Travelocity has a "Book Your Roundtrip Flight Now!" option prominently displayed on its home page. The regular "Book A Flight" page gives the choice of being flexible on times for a selected date but not during a date range. I couldn't find a mechanism to let you check for the lowest current published fares on specific routes, but the "Fare Watcher Email" feature lets you monitor fares on up to five routings. When the fare goes up or down $25, you are alerted, and the system also creates "Your Personal Fare Watcher Page" to which you can return at any time. There you will find the current lowest fare on your selected routes and the airlines that are offering it, along with a link to the fare rules governing the fares. In addition to the fare alert, you can sign up for a free travel newsletter. There is a link to a separate booking engine for consolidator fares.

1Travel.com

www.onetravel.com

This site is aimed squarely at the budget traveler. It also prides itself on its information resources, which include regular contributions from guru Terry Trippler. In addition, there is an integrated search engine for consolidator fares.

American Express

travel.americanexpress.com

Despite its upscale image, the American Express site rates highly for its usefulness to bargain hunters. It is powered by the GetThere/ITN booking engine, one of the best.

ByeByeNow

www.byebyenow.com

TravelByUs

www.travelbyus.com

These two agencies are going head to head for dominance in the so-called "clicks and mortar" arena. In addition to an on-line booking engine, both boast an extensive network of store-front agencies where you can pick up tickets and (will wonders never cease?) talk to a human being. Of course, the same can be said of American Express and other old-line travel chains that have entered the e-commerce arena.

biztravel.com

www.biztravel.com

Affiliated with the Rosenbluth chain of travel agencies, this site asks for car and hotel preferences as well as the purpose of your trip before allowing you to price flights. The site does have some nice information resources.

Etravnet

www.etravnet.com

In addition to a straightforward booking engine, Etravnet offers HaggleWithUs.com, a patent-pending service that allows you to bargain in real time for a flight (or other product) you have booked. The catch is you must commit to buying the ticket before the haggling process can begin. The main site also has a well-developed cruise booking engine.

Other online travel agencies

In addition to the sites profiled above, there is an ever-increasing number of other players, large and small. Some of them piggyback on the big sites mentioned above, using their booking engines and adding their own bells and whistles. Others have a leisure vacation focus and treat airline bookings as something of an extra-added attraction to their site. Here are just a few of them, along with the briefest of comments:

Airlines of the Web (www.flyaow.com)
> This site lets you look for charters as well as scheduled flights.

Atevo (www.atevo.com)
> Extensive resources, tips, and bulletin board sections.

CheapAirlines (www.cheapairlines.com)
> This site says you can book a flight in "4 short steps."

Leisure Planet (www.leisureplanet.com)
> Specializes in international leisure travel.

Traveler's Net (www.travelersnet.com)
> They offer a rebate on tickets booked on their site.

TravelHero (www.travelhero.com)
> Claims the "largest database of hotels, motels, bed and breakfasts, inns and other lodging on the Internet today."

Travelscape (www.travelscape.com)
> Travelscape uses Expedia's search engine and allows you to search for air-hotel packages.

Trip.com (www.trip.com)
> Owned by Galileo, a computerized reservations system provider.

Uniglobe (www.uniglobe.com)
> The online presence of a major chain.

Yahoo Travel (travel.yahoo.com)
> Uses the Travelocity booking engine.

The Empire strikes back, part II

Apparently, the airlines just can't stand the thought of someone else making money that they could pocket themselves. At press time, the five largest U.S. airlines had announced that they were going into the online travel agency business for themselves.

The planned site is dubbed Orbitz.com and it should be online by the time you read this. Although Orbitz will theoretically be independent of the airlines that own it, the big online travel agencies charge that Orbitz will offer web-only fares that will undercut everyone else. Storefront agencies aren't any happier about the development, and the American Society of Travel Agents (ASTA) has asked the government to investigate. The Department of Justice and the Department of Transportation have both announced they are studying the issue. It will be interesting to see how this shakes out.

Consolidator booking engines

For the last several years, consolidators have been starting up web sites at an ever-increasing rate. Usually these sites serve as the electronic equivalent of a business card or newspaper ad; to make inquiries and book a flight you generally (but not always) have to contact the consolidator by phone. Some consolidator web sites let you book online and a few forego direct contact altogether and handle bookings entirely online.

The next logical step would seem to be booking engines for consolidator flights that would allow you to search for flights and make bookings online without ever speaking to a human being. There have been some attempts at this, but at this writing the only site I could find that claims to search for fares at many consolidators is TravelHUB (www.travelhub.com). TravelHUB claims a database of over 500 consolidators and discounts as high as 40 percent.

Your best bet for finding consolidator fares on the web is to consult the list of consolidators in Chapter Six and visit their individual sites.

Should I book on the Internet?

Good question. And as is the case with so many questions, the answer is, "It depends."

There are some cases in which there is no alternative to booking on the Internet. Many of the airlines offer certain deals only on their Internet web sites. Book online (or on the phone directly with the airline) or forego the special fare. If the fare is especially attractive, then it certainly makes sense to book online. In other cases, the fare deal quoted by an airline on its web site may be available elsewhere (in other words, from a travel agent), but the airline may offer a special inducement, such as additional frequent flyer miles, for booking online. Again, if there is no difference in the fare, why not grab the goodies?

I have mixed emotions about these deals because they seem such a calculated attempt to wean the traveling public away from travel agents. The dark, conspiratorial, paranoid side of my nature tells me that when the airlines have made it difficult for the average Joe to find a travel agent willing to book air travel, these special fares and extra goodies will evaporate. Remember our earlier discussion about how the major airlines reduce fares when a low-fare competitor enters the market, only to boost them again when the low-fare choice goes belly up?

Still, the airlines come up with some pretty mouth-watering deals from time to time. If you decide to spurn them on principle, good for you. If you're like the rest of us, you'll probably succumb, at least some of the time. I won't hold it against you.

Mind you, so far we've been talking about fares that are offered on airline web sites and clearly marked as special offers or sales. Booking a "regular" ticket on an airline web site, even one that proclaims it offers a "low fare finder" option, is problematic for reasons cited at the beginning of this chapter. In that case, there is an excellent chance that an experienced travel agent can beat the airline's quote. And, of course, the airline isn't going to remind you that it has a low-fare competitor on the route.

Purchasing tickets from the online travel agencies is yet another matter. As we've seen, offline travel agents can very often beat their online brethren, which after all are designed to come up with a fast answer, not necessarily the best answer. One possible approach is to use the online sites as a way of ballparking the fare and then call a travel agent or two to see if they can beat it. I have some concerns about this approach because a travel agent's time is valuable and I certainly don't want to encourage you to join the legions of "tire-kickers" who are already making travel agents' lives miserable.

If you do adopt this approach, I would encourage you to do the following. When the travel agent quotes the better fare, book it with that agent. When you find a travel agent who consistently gives you better deals, give your business to that agent.

Remember, too, that when an actual ticket is involved, the online agent will add a fee for delivery of that ticket. That, and any other fees, should be factored in when you are making fare comparisons.

Keeping current

One thing the Internet does well is provide information. If you know how to prevent information overload, the 'Net can serve as a distant early warning system of air fare news you can use. I've already mentioned the weekly e-mails the airlines send out. Here are some more ways to keep current:

Portals

An Internet portal is a web site that you choose as the default page to load when you launch your Internet browser. Companies such as Yahoo, Netscape, Microsoft Network, Excite, and many others are eager to become your Internet portal. The beauty of portals is that they can be customized to provide you with information tailored to your needs and interests, everything from the weather in Paris, to the latest stock quotes and sports scores, to air fares. The "My Yahoo" portal, which I use, lets me track current "lowest" air fares to several destinations of my choosing via Travelocity. I am sure most other portals offer similar services. If not, it's an easy matter to switch portals; your Internet browser has a feature that lets you specify which page it summons up when you launch it.

The lowest fares given (at least on my portal) should be taken with a grain of salt. For example, Orlando is a destination in which I am interested. Lately, my portal has been telling me that the lowest roundtrip fare is $190, plus taxes and passenger facility charges. I just booked a flight for $164 roundtrip, *including* taxes and PFCs. No big secret to this; I simply used the common sense strategies outlined in this book.

What the fare tracking mechanism on my portal *can* do, however, is alert me to major changes in the market. If, for example, I see the fare to Orlando drop to $150, I'll know something is afoot. Perhaps a fare war has started, perhaps this is the time to plan ahead. (See Ploy #2 in Chapter One.)

News searches

There's an easy way to keep up on the latest news about airline fare sales and fare wars. Simply type the following URL into your Internet browser's address window: http://search.news.yahoo.com/search/news?p=airline+fare +sales

Better yet, enter it as a new bookmark in your browser's bookmark file or folder. This will take you to a list of the latest news stories from major wire services and PR outlets that contain the keywords "airline," "fare," and "sales." If an airline has announced a special deal, there's an excellent chance it will show up here. If a fare war has broken out in Los Angeles, there's a good chance some news hound has written it up. By the way, you can alter the terms after the "news?p=" in the URL to search for any topic that interests you.

Destinations Unlimited

This nifty service (www.air-fare.com) tracks published fares from and to 50 major cities in the United States in up to eight categories, from lowest excursion fare to lowest regular first class. For each fare, the site provides the airlines offering it and abbreviated fare codes. This information will enable you to call a travel agent and nail the exact fare (assuming you can be flexible on dates and the fare is not sold out).

The site also calls out major fare cuts by city and what it calls "air fare goofs," which occur when airlines make typos while posting fares to the computerized reservations systems. One example cited was a $2,000 first-class ticket for $200. The information is updated daily. There is also a booking engine on the site.

If you live in or near one of the cities listed and are traveling to one of the other 49, this should be your first stop when researching fares.

Chapter Nine

Becoming a Travel Agent

Some of you may have seen ads in *The Wall Street Journal*, on late-night infomercials, or elsewhere extolling the benefits of becoming a travel agent — instantly — and using the photo ID card that comes along with your newfound (and rather pricey) identity to qualify for special "to-the-trade-only" deals and discounts. As with so much in the world of marketing hype there is both more and less here than meets the eye. In this chapter, I will try to give you a overview of what is and is not feasible. This whole area is fraught with controversy (especially in the travel agent community) and misunderstanding (especially in the press). So I will try to lay out the facts, as I see them, without getting anyone too mad at me.

To begin with, let's draw a basic but very important distinction between two kinds of "instant" travel agents — referral travel agents and what I will call independent, home-based travel agents.

Referral travel agents

Most of the "become a travel agent today!" deals you see advertised involve becoming a "referral agent." The companies offering these deals may say you'll be an "associate agent" or an "independent agent" or something else, but you'll be a referral agent nonetheless. That means that your job is simply to *refer* potential customers to the sponsoring agency — get them to call a toll-free number where the agency's "inside agents" will take care of closing the sale and handle the booking details. In exchange for providing this service, you receive a portion of the commission earned by the agency. So far, there's is nothing new or controversial in this. It's called "bird-dogging" and has been going on in the travel industry for years. What's new and controversial is the aggressive packaging and marketing of the concept that has occurred in recent years.

To further complicate things, there are two basic types of referral agent programs. One incorporates a multi-level marketing component, whereby you not only receive compensation for signing up new agents but participate in the commissions generated through their activities as well. To some observers this looks uncomfortably like a pyramid scheme. Consequently, agencies in this category have been attacked on legal grounds. Some have been outlawed in several states. Others have gone out of business as a result of the legal actions taken against them, only to resurface after modifying their programs. Not surprisingly, they have been attacked vigorously by travel agents and the travel trade press. In short, they have been unstable.

Another type of referral agency has been more successful. These agencies are multi-level to the extent that they pay a bounty or referral fee if you sign up new agents, but they don't have any of those complicated formulas that promise that you'll earn income though a "downline" of the agents you've signed up. They, too, have been controversial, although they have actually managed to gain some grudging respect from the travel trade press if not from the rank and file travel agent. These are the kinds of agency I will talk about here.

How they work

Referral agencies have remarkable similarities. It's almost as if they all worked off the same business and marketing plans. Here are some of the hallmarks of a referral agency:
- *A $495 sign-up fee.* Most, maybe all, referral agencies will charge you $495 to become one of their agents. If they charged $500 or more, they would trigger much stricter regulatory oversight, a fact that raises eyebrows

among more cynical observers. In addition, you will probably have to pay an annual fee of $99 or more.

- *A photo ID card.* A big part of the marketing lure is the photo ID card they issue to their agents. This card, you are told, will unlock the door to discounts and privileges available only to travel agents. This is why referral agencies are called "card mills" (the term is an insult) by many professional travel agents.

- *A bounty on new agents.* Referral agencies are constantly looking for more agents. They will pay you anywhere from $75 to $200 for each new one you recruit for them.

- *"Selling" travel.* Most referral agencies encourage you to talk up the joys of travel in general, talk up their agency in particular, and pass out to all and sundry a business card (which usually costs you extra) with their 800 number. The card contains your "PIN number," a unique identifier that assures you get your commission. One of the most attractive aspects of this deal is that once a customer has your PIN attached to his or her name, you receive a cut of all that person's travel in perpetuity.

- *Low commissions on airline tickets.* This is not too surprising since the commissions the agencies receive from the airlines are so paltry.

- *Fixed commissions on everything else.* Most referral agencies "assume" that the commission is always 10% and pay you a portion of that commission (typically half) on everything other than air. In fact, the agency may be earning a commission as high as 17% from some suppliers. In this case, the referring agent gets 5%, while the agency itself gets 12%.

- *Agent-only discounts.* Most referral agencies offer special in-house deals to their own agents. These are deals you purchase through the agency, as opposed to deals you request from a supplier using your ID card.

Is it a good deal?

Viewed strictly as a money-making proposition, the answer is probably no. Let's run the numbers, as they were laid out in a recent, highly favorable article in *Inc.* magazine about Global Travel International (GTI), the most prominent referral agency. According to the article, GTI has 22,000 agents and 1998 sales of $100 million. That would suggest that the *average* agent books $4,545 a year. At a 5% commission, the agent is getting $227. (Actually, the average figure would probably be lower since airline tickets pay such a low commission and probably account for at least some of the typical agent's bookings.) In other words, the agent is losing money on the deal for the first three years and clearing $116, after total expenses, in the fourth year. Of course, if an agent is responsible for referring $10,000 in business the first year (again, assuming an across-the-board 5% effective commission) the card pays for itself in year one. In succeeding years, the agent would only need to generate $2,000 in bookings to break even.

The other major way to get a return on your investment is to recruit others as independent agents. As noted earlier, commissions on new sign-ups range from $75 to $200. Some agents do very well just talking others into joining.

I suspect, however, that few people join these agencies to get rich. Even the management of referral agencies will admit, off the record, that none of their agents are making a living doing this. The few who join wanting to be full- or even part-time travel agents no doubt soon realize their mistake and seek out the more business-like deals available to home-based travel agents, which I'll discuss a bit later.

Most people who sign up do so for the benefits — real, imagined, or a bit of both. When I pointed out to a salesperson for one referral agency that I would be hard-pressed to recoup my investment on commissions, she countered that "most of our members pay for the card in one weekend just with the hotel discounts." (Assuming a three-day stay and a 50% discount, that suggests these people are used to paying $330 a night for a hotel room!) Looked at that way, becoming a referral agent is somewhat akin to joining a travel club — except it costs $495 instead of $50 or $60 the first year and $99 or $150 a year thereafter instead of the same $50 or $60. So the question then becomes, just how good are those discounts?

Let's start with air fare since that's the focus of this book. First of all, don't expect to wave your referral agent ID at an airline reservationist and get a discount. Travel agents *do* get discounts from the airlines but there's a lot of paperwork involved, a higher standard of proof (in terms of establishing that you are, indeed, a travel agent), and restrictions on travel dates. Even then, the travel agent flying on a reduced fare is subject to being bumped if the flight fills up. A lot of travel agents, in fact, think these discounts are more trouble than they're worth.

What you might — repeat, *might* — get from an airline with your ID card is a complimentary upgrade to first or business class on a flight for which you hold a paid-for coach ticket. I know it can be done because I've done it myself. You show your ID card to the gate agent and ask if there are any "courtesy upgrades" available. Now as you might expect, this is the sort of thing that gets "real" travel agents especially hot under the collar. Because they complained so loudly, the airlines (the domestic ones at least) have been getting a lot savvier about travel agent ID cards. Most of them have declared that they will only accept the IATAN card as proof that the holder is a travel agent. IATAN is the International Airlines Travel Agent Network, an accrediting organization. Its procedures, while subject to potential abuse, tend to assure that the holders of its cards are actually employed in the travel agency business. Because of the furor over this ploy, the referral agencies themselves seem to have pulled back from promoting this as a benefit. Still, the anecdotal evidence is that it can still be pulled off, by some people some of the time. For some people, this ploy can raise ethical questions. Others claim that using a referral agency ID in this fashion is technically illegal, although I can't imagine an airline pressing charges. At most, you can expect to be humiliated when a knowledgeable gate agent turns you down and gives you a piece of his or her mind. Still, a business class seat can be mighty tempting. My guess is that this potential benefit lures a lot of referral agents.

Yes, you can get discounts on hotel rates and rental cars by flashing your referral agent ID, but these discounts are not really "travel agent discounts" like the ones extended to holders of the IATAN card. Rather, they are similar in nature to discounts given to travel club members or members of groups like AARP and AAA. I have seen no evidence that the discounts referral agents get are any better than those you can get from a travel club or a "half-priced" hotel program. I'm not saying the evidence doesn't exist, I'm just saying I haven't seen it.

The "for our agents only" deals on cruises, hotel packages, and the like are something else again. Some of these can be quite attractive. Typically they are for mid-market products in destinations most popular with the masses of American tourists — Florida, Colorado, Las Vegas, Hawaii, Mexico, and the Caribbean. You are unlikely to find any deals on luxury properties (like hotels on Venice's Grand Canal) or niche products (like trekking in the Himalayas). You are more likely to find cruise deals on Carnival than on Seabourne.

One of the major problems with referral agencies, in my opinion, is that their infrastructure sometimes has trouble keeping up with their marketing. In other words, they sign up so many agents that they have trouble answering the flood of phone calls that result. This can be particularly embarrassing when you have handed out a business card to a friend who calls you a week later to complain that "that number you gave me is always busy." Long waits on hold and unmet promises to return calls are other problems. The agencies are aware of these problems and seem to make a good faith effort to solve them. Once you get through to the agency, the inside agents all seem to be well-trained, efficient, and reasonably accomplished at searching out the best fare. If you have a straightforward ticketing request, you are likely to get good service. At least that has been my experience in dealing with these agencies.

Finally, it must be said that for some people there is the thrill that they are "beating the system" even if, in their heart of hearts, they know they're not really. Clearly these deals have some appeal to a great many people. As noted, GTI claims 22,000 agents and says 90% of them rejoin after the first year.

Becoming a referral agent will make the most sense if:
- *You travel a lot.* Those hotel discounts do add up, although it may take you more than a weekend to recoup your investment.
- *You are an upscale traveler.* If you are used to staying in $300-a-night hotels, the discounts may be attractive. And if you regularly travel in business class, getting a break on a single trip could make this deal worthwhile to you.
- *You are willing to sign up a few new agents.* If this is the sort of thing you're good at, you can actually make some money.
- *You are bold enough to try for the free upgrade every time you fly.* Quite frankly, this one bothers me enough that I haven't done it in quite a while. Others clearly don't share my qualms.

Becoming a referral agent

In spite of all the above (and as you may have guessed), I am a referral agent myself. I can make the claim that I joined in the spirit of professional research, but I joined nonetheless. I am not recommending that you join, and I am certainly not encouraging you to misrepresent yourself in any way. However, if you are interested in pursuing the matter further, here is contact information for Global Travel International which charges $495 to become one of their agents. I cannot guarantee your satisfaction, but GTI has been the subject of flattering coverage by *Inc., USA Today,* and *The Wall Street Journal.* For what it's worth, it is located in Florida, which has fairly strict laws governing travel agencies and travel promoters.

Global Travel International
2300 Maitland Center Parkway, Suite 140
Maitland, FL 32751
(800) 715-4440
www.gtiweb.com
Referral PIN: 42468001

If you do look into joining, be sure to ask about special two-for-one deals that let you and a spouse or friend join for the price of a single membership. Referral agencies frequently run this type of promotion. Less frequently, they run "lifetime membership" offers. Make sure to ask and don't be afraid to bargain a bit by mentioning that you are considering another agency as well. If you supply the PIN number given above when and if you join, I will receive a commission — at least I *should* receive a commission. Don't use the PIN if you don't want to. I'm sure they'll still let you sign up. I should also hasten to add that this is the only agency mentioned in this book in which I have any financial interest.

Home-based travel agents

Independent, home-based travel agents (as I call them) differ from referral agents in one very important respect: they do all the work of researching fares, closing sales, and making bookings with suppliers that referral agents avoid. In return, they get a much higher share of the commission. They may even get it all.

Home-based agents are similar to referral agents in that, for the most part, they function as outside sales representatives for a "host agency" with which they split commissions. Sometimes they get as much as 70% or 80% of the actual commission (not an "assumed" 10% commission). The primary reason to ally with a host agency is to be able to sell airline tickets. That's because only accredited, bonded travel agencies can print airline tickets. However, there are a great many other travel products — notably tours and cruises — that in many instances can be sold directly by independent home-based agents without involving a host agency. In these cases, the home-based agent earns the entire commission, often several hundred dollars at a time.

Home-based agents also look a lot more like a business than their referral agent counterparts. Typically, they operate under a business name that is different from the name of their host agency and different, as well, from their own name. In other words, "Mary's Trips 'n' Travel" as opposed to Mary Smith. Most of them also have a business checking account, which further adds to their identity as a "travel agency." In most important respects they *are* a travel agency.

Is it a good deal?

Becoming a home-based agent simply to save money on your own air fare is probably not a great idea. Commissions on air fare, as noted earlier, are low and getting lower. There's not much to split. Then, too, many host agencies that work with independent home-based agents have their own sign-up fees, which can be higher than those charged by referral agencies. These companies, after all, are looking for serious sellers of travel, not dabblers. There are agencies that will take you on for less, even for free, but if you are selling only one airline ticket every couple of months — to yourself — they may decide not to keep you on.

There are two exceptions to this rule. If you are buying consolidator tickets, there is no need to join a host agency. As long as you have a business checking account that sounds like it belongs to a travel agency, you should have no trouble finding a consolidator who will work with you. In fact, I strongly suspect that there are consolidators who will sell you a ticket anyway, just as long as your check's good and especially if you pay in cash. But ideally you should have checks that say something like "Sam's Travel." If they say "Sam's Enterprises," a consolidator may give you the benefit of the doubt, but if they say "Sam's Dry Cleaners," you may have trouble convincing a consolidator you sell travel.

The savings you realize on consolidator tickets for yourself and your family will quickly pay for the minor expenses of setting up a small home-based travel business. If you also sell tickets to friends you can make some money on the side. Here is a simple strategy for doing that: Tell your friends to find the best deal they can get on an international ticket and ask them to give you a chance to beat it. If you can find a consolidator with a lower quote, split the difference 50/50 with your friend. You don't have to tell him how much you're paying, just quote a fare that's half way between what you'll pay the consolidator and what your friend would pay the airline. It's a win-win situation.

241

The other exception is when you own a small business that has more than $25,000 or $30,000 a year in air fare expenses. In that case, setting up an in-house travel agency can have financial advantages, in addition to providing nice perks to both the owner and employees.

These observations, remember, apply to the rather limited situation of the person who is seeking to save money on air fare alone. If, on the other hand, you would like to actually make some money by building a full- or part-time business around something you love — travel — as well as save money on your own travel, then becoming an independent home-based travel agent should have great appeal. Not only will you be putting money in the bank, you'll be saving money (in the form of commissions) on your own travel. What's more, a great deal of the travel you do will become a tax-deductible expense, since it is business-related. With a modicum of effort you can qualify for the IATAN card. In this situation, any savings you realize on air fare is gravy.

Even a part-time home-based travel business can pay terrific dividends. For example, my wife and I once put together a group for a luxury cruise aboard a magnificent four-masted clipper ship. In exchange for our efforts, the cruise line gave us a free berth. The commissions paid for the other berth, and we had money left over to put in the bank.

Becoming an independent home-based travel agent is not for everyone, but if the idea appeals to you I would encourage you to investigate further. You will probably be surprised at how easy it is to get started — and you don't have to spend a fortune either. For more information, visit the Home-Based Travel Agent Resource Center on the Internet at:

http://www.HomeTravelAgency.com

Chapter Ten

Further Reading

It is not possible to pack absolutely everything into this book, so I've tried to provide the information that would be most helpful to the most people. However, there is much more information out there and that is what this chapter is all about. Several of my other books, for example, expand upon themes touched upon in this one. All of them are available at finer bookstores everywhere or directly from The Intrepid Traveler.

Air Courier Bargains: How To Travel World-Wide For Next To Nothing is the book that launched my travel writing career. It is now in its seventh edition and includes an extensive annotated directory of every courier company in the world. I included basic information about U.S. courier companies in this book, but *Air Courier Bargains* provides much more detailed information about each of them, including charts showing flight frequency, length of stay, airlines flown, and so forth. It also provides similar in-depth coverage of courier companies in England, Hong Kong, Singapore, Japan, Australia, New Zealand, Argentina, and so on. Remember, as long as you have a valid passport, your courier trip can originate anywhere!

Air Travel's Bargain Basement: The International Directory of Consolidators, Bucket Shops and Other Sources of Discount Travel contains all the listings I didn't have space for here. In addition to listing over 500 sources of cheap tickets in the United States (helpfully cross-referenced by location and destinations served), this information-packed directory also lists consolidators and discount travel agencies around the world. Web sites are included where available.

Home-Based Travel Agent is a 400-page manual that outlines the steps needed to set up a home-based travel agency on a shoe-string and make it succeed. Those of you who are serious about going into the travel business might want to invest in the Home-Based Travel Agent home study course offered by the Home-Based Travel Agent Resource Center. The course includes *Home-Based Travel Agent* and a number of other helpful manuals. You will find full details on the course on the Internet at:

http://www.HomeTravelAgency.com

Periodicals

I am listing here a number of magazines that I feel offer excellent value for the dollar. Of course, a dollar spent on a magazine is a dollar that can't be spent on an airline ticket; but most of these publications will pay for themselves fairly quickly. These are not "wish books" like *Travel & Leisure* and *Conde Nast Traveler*, filled with lush photographs of luxury hideaways you can't afford. Rather they concern themselves, in various ways, with the nitty gritty details of wringing the best deal possible from the travel marketplace.

Best Fares

1301 South Bowen Road, Suite 490
Arlington, TX 76013
(800) 880-1234
www.bestfares.com
Monthly; $59.95 a year.

Tom Parsons' obsession with air fares has paid off big time in this glossy monthly. Your annual subscription also gets you into the Best Fares Travel Club and a half-priced hotel program. Another subscriber benefit is access to a members-only section of their web site. My favorite feature of *Best Fares* is the "Snooze You Lose" fare alerts on the web site. If you pay by credit card, they will automatically renew your subscription each year.

Consumer Reports Travel Letter

P.O. Box 53629
Boulder, CO 80322-3629
(800) 234-1970
Monthly; $39 a year, $59 for two years.

This 24-page newsletter is published by the same folks who bring you *Consumer Reports* magazine. The readership seems to be fairly upscale and the editorial focus is not so much on budget travel as it is on getting the best value for the dollars you do spend. If you're looking for someone who will measure the distance between seats in every airline or spend weeks figuring out which car rental company offers the best deal, this is the newsletter for you. A disturbing anti-travel agent attitude has crept into their editorial policy since the estimable editor Ed Perkins hung up his traveling shoes, but they still can't be beat for crunching the numbers.

InsideFlyer

4715-C Town Center Drive
Colorado Springs, CO 80916-4709
(719) 597-8880
www.insideflyer.com
Monthly; $36 a year, $59 for two years.

Randy Petersen is to frequent flyer miles what Tom Parsons is to air fares. His is the publication of choice for those who obsess about their frequent flyer status. If you've been gathering miles willy nilly, without the slightest idea of how to spend them, let alone manage them, this magazine will set you straight. If you order online, you'll be rewarded with — what else? — frequent flyer miles.

Jax Fax

397 Post Road
Darien, CT 06820-1413
(203) 655-8746
Monthly; $15 a year; $24 for two years.

This trade publication, aimed at travel agents, consists primarily of listing after listing of "net" fares offered by consolidators to the trade. For the budget traveler it is an inexpensive way of keeping up to date on the going rate to destinations around the world. If you have read *Home-Based Travel Agent*, of course, you can get these low, low net fares for yourself.

Rudy Maxa's Traveler

1746 N Street NW
Washington, DC 20036
(800) 387-8025
www.savtravnewsletter.com
Monthly; $54 a year.

Rudy Maxa, host of Public Radio's popular *Savvy Traveler* program, now produces a monthly newsletter. It's not simply a rehash of material from the show, but a freestanding cornucopia of budget travel news, tips, and techniques. Rudy combines the nitty gritty of getting the best deal with a sense of fun and excitement — which is what travel's all about, isn't it? Thanks to first-rate writing leavened with wit, this one manages to be entertaining as well as informative.

Subject Index

Visit

Family of Web Sites

http://www.IntrepidTraveler.com

Our main site with a complete catalog of money-saving,
horizon-expanding books, plus our online travel magazine.

http//www.BeatTheAirlines.com

Learn how to beat the airlines at their own game on a site
that helps make sure you never pay full fare again.

http://www.HomeTravelAgency.com

Join the thousands of people who are earning good money
and free travel as home-based travel agents.

http://www.TheOtherOrlando.com

The site devoted to the wonderful world outside the
Magic Kingdom.